IN JUSTICE

IN JUSTICE
WOMEN AND GLOBAL ECONOMICS

Ann-Cathrin Jarl

Fortress Press
Minneapolis

IN JUSTICE
Women in Global Economics

Cover design: Marti Naughton
Cover image: "Two Figures Holding Up Buildings," by José Ortega, © 2002 The Stock Illustration Source. Used by permission.

The paper used in this publication meets the minimum requirements of American National Standard for Information Sciences—Permanence of Paper for Printed Library Materials, ANSI Z329.48–1984.

Manufactured in the U.S.A.
08   07   06   05   04   03   1   2   3   4   5   6   7   8   9   10

CONTENTS

Part Three: Economic Justice

PREFACE

Although the desperately poor comprise half the earth's population, they remain largely invisible to economists and economic planners. Yet when millions of willing and capable people cannot feed themselves or provide for their basic needs through their own work, it presents steep challenges and tough questions to the global economic system, to economic theory, and to thoughtful people everywhere. How can these life-and-death issues of justice and well-being, of material well-being, become part of our economic thought and life? What does economic justice mean today?

Addressing these critical questions today entails an extensive encounter with the reigning economic paradigm—neoclassical economics—and analysis of economics as theory, as science, and as a living practice. It also entails a sound ethical analysis of our economic behavior, proposals for alternative economic models, and benchmarks for how we define economic justice.

In this work I search for a new framework for economics and the ethical criteria by which economic ideas can be assessed. Especially in light of the ongoing presence of massive poverty around the world and its disproportionate impact on women, I highlight the important insights and most promising ideas of feminist economists, feminist ethicists, and feminist liberation theologians. For in fact it is from women, and especially women in poor countries, that some of the most important thinking about renewing economics has risen.

In challenging economics regarding issues of gender and justice, I hope to get beyond the merely political debate and to deepen thought about the ethical dimension of doing economics. I also challenge feminists to draw more deeply from critical theory and to recognize that—despite the necessary postmodern emphasis on particularities and context—poverty, oppression, and injustice are global and must be tackled in light of commonalities of people and structures everywhere. Feminist theory has developed an inductive method that can help to reorient our understanding of justice as a process.

In the first part I introduce the chief concepts of neoclassical economic theory. Then I show how feminist theorists have critiqued the now-triumphant market model, especially as it affects women. An alternative economics, as pioneered by Indian economists Bina Agarwal and Gita Sen, is presented in the third chapter. It centers around issues of power, equality, rights, and basic needs. I focus particularly on how ethical analysis has become an intrinsic part of feminist economics.

The second part of this work takes up challenges of feminist ethics explicitly. I show how critical theory, ideological analysis, narrative, and liberation thinking can be allies in forging a deeper understanding of injustice, oppression, and societal dynamics.

Finally, in the third part I try to draw all these strands together. I ask, what then can feminist economics and feminist ethics really contribute to our idea of economic justice? I argue that the fundamental ethical criterion and measure for economic theory and practice is provision for basic human needs. It is the benchmark, the foundation and fulcrum, for improving economic justice today and for bringing the claims of justice to the world of markets.

This is a work in Christian social ethics, and my stance there is partly strategic. Christian faith encompasses many people throughout the world, and I want to make them more aware of how Christian ethics, feminism, and economics interact. But further, I hope also to show that Christian ethics and theology offer important values that can strengthen the position of women and the poor everywhere in their search for justice and well-being in the global household.

PART ONE

FEMINIST ECONOMICS

1

MARKET ECONOMICS
AND FEMINIST ECONOMICS

Six vital areas of interest for feminist ethics—gender, equality, rights, power, objectivity, and experience—hold promise for assessing and rethinking economic theory and practice. They are largely found in feminist economic thought, so Part One of this work explores them. I first explore the feminist economic critique of neoclassical economic theory and the values inherent in it.

In fact, feminist economics arises precisely in response to the traditional, and still reigning, economic paradigm.[1] To set the stage, therefore, we recall some of the main assumptions and tenets of the contemporary economic model, which can be roughly termed *neoclassical economics.* The main picture is familiar to most Westerners, at least, and can be briefly sketched as follows:

Market Economics

What is economic theory all about? The word *economic* goes back to the Greek *oikos,* meaning household, and *nomos,* meaning law. *Oikonomia* thus denotes rules or law of the household. Economics is about how we manage our household, our community. Its focus can be the behavior and dynamics of a literal household or individuals or a single firm (microeconomics). But it can also focus on the aggregate behavior of households or firms as they operate in the social system of an entire region or nation (macroeconomics). Economics searches for behavioral patterns in human exchanges of value.

Classical economics supposes that the resources exchanged—be they raw materials, land, capital, services, or goods—are limited. Yet human needs and desires are not. This hard fact underlies the modern concept of economics, which economic Richard Lipsey defines as "the study of the use of scarce resources to satisfy unlimited human wants."[2] In its contemporary or neoclassical formulation, economics analyzes exchange behavior through such key concepts as the market mechanism, labor, scarcity, supply and demand, and goods.

The prime focus in neoclassical economics is the "market," as an important object of both theoretical and practical study.[3] The market is any site of exchange. In the market, at least theoretically, transactions take place between free, rational, and "utility-maximizing" agents. That is, economists assume, for the sake of analysis, that humans bring full knowledge, clarity, and freedom to their transactions and that human agents seek thereby to increase or maximize their self-interest, however they understand that "utility." In theory, independent markets can do anything that agents want. Adam Smith, the founding father of Western economics, theorized that, left to its own inner logic, the market would be able to supply what people wanted and organize it all in the best way possible. The supply of and demand for goods and services would fluctuate to meet people's desires as reflected in the prices they are willing to pay for the goods and services, relative to each other. Competition among both suppliers and buyers regulated prices continuously. This price mechanism, Smith argued, operated spontaneously in markets, like an "invisible hand," to maximize benefits to each economic actor or agent.[4]

Adam Smith's foundational market concept thus included both an analytical and a moral dimension. But Smith lived insulated in a homogenous Western culture and assumed that a universal moral understanding actually existed and was sufficient to provide moral guidelines for economics. In reality, this "pure" form of the market does not exist, if it ever did. All markets are constrained not only by lack of knowledge or clarity in the actors but also by political decisions, which regulate how markets function. And the degree of regulation varies considerably. In addition, opinions about the degree of regulation needed to optimize the functions of the market also vary.

Through the price mechanism, Smith argued, the market is instrumental in the distribution of goods and services and increases the utility of those goods and services. The market is the place where what has been produced under the auspices of perfect competition is offered for sale. In theory, whatever happens with economics is related to what happens in the market, where "free" and "rational" individuals meet.

When economists refer to the market, it seems like reference is made to a well-known and univocal concept. In fact, however, there are many types of markets, and they differ in kind; there is the market of goods and services, the labor market, the informal market, the financial market, global markets, and different kinds of black markets.

The markets that we are most familiar with in our daily lives are those for goods and services, and what happens in this market is a major topic in economic theory. How, why, and when do people make decisions to act in this market? How are goods and services provided?

In the market for production of goods and services, we find Adam Smith's baker, who bakes his bread to be able to provide for his family. Because people make the choice to buy his bread, he continues to bake it. In this market the ideal or model economic person operates to maximize his utility or benefit. Here marginal utility is studied; here the right price is established. Supply and demand and competition are key components in theories about this market. Resources that go into the economy are analyzed, and the political decisions that regulate the market are considered as well.

The production of goods and services and their exchange also occupy many feminist economists engaged in development work. The scope of markets even within this one market is immense. For instance, the kind of work that organizations like the Self-Employed Women's Association have performed in India to help women enter the local markets and support themselves is distinctly different from the market where transnational corporations operate globally to maximize profit. There is virtually no comparison of these two markets in size, range, or character of assets, credit, mobility in time and space, and innovation.

To most people, the labor market will be familiar. It is through the labor market that most people are able to obtain resources, usually money. Though many difficulties attach to careers and career options, the labor market is where most people must achieve success. That is why some people are not making it in this world—they cannot get jobs. The labor market may be closed or restricted to them because of their race, sex, education, language, class, nationality, lack of experience, or some other reason, known or unknown to them. Paid labor is a cost for those who need goods produced and services performed, and hence firms and producers are unlikely to hire more labor than they need to.

Labor, of course, is only one of the many assets needed to manufacture goods and provide services. Other necessary assets include land, capital, and natural resources. Producers have a vested interest in keeping all costs as low as possible.[5]

The fastest-growing market today is the financial market. Technological innovations and electronic communications around the world are helpmates in this growth. Other factors are the lifting of various kinds of national restrictions or levies pertaining to trade, ease of currency exchange, lifting of interest ceilings, and, of course, access to the market.[6] More and more, people in the Western world are growing familiar with the financial market for personal reasons: to increase their assets and to secure their future and retirement. But the vast majority of the world's people have no idea what the financial market is about.

Institutions that collect and maintain large funds, like retirement funds, insurance premiums, and labor union dues, are also major investors in the financial markets and are major actors there. Transparency in the financial markets has increased with modern technology and standardization of international trading, but actual trade within the market has its specialists and is closed to most people. The volume of trade in the financial market is quickly outgrowing trade of goods and services.[7] The chief working tools of the financial market are its electronic trading mechanisms. The speed in trade is high, often extremely high, and the need for a workforce is limited, while the profit and risk tend to be high. Here, no goods, commodities, or services (with the exception of financial services) as such are produced. Many developing nations have difficulty knowing about these markets or finding ways to access or control them.

One of the leaders in international financial markets, George Soros, owns and directs Soros Fund Management in New York City. He critiques the universally accepted laissez-faire policies in economics and suggests instead that it should be called "market fundamentalism," which he says has detrimental consequences for the open society that he favors. Soros writes:

> Nobody would deny that we live in a global economy. It is characterized not only by free trade but even more by the free movement of capital. Capital is more mobile than labor or land; and financial capital is even more mobile than direct investment. Financial capital will move wherever it receives the best treatment. Generally it will avoid taxation and regulation so the economies of individual countries are not only interdependent but they are also dependent on the need to attract and retain capital. That is why the global economy can be described as the global capitalist system. Capital is in the driver's seat and countries which are at the center of the global capitalist systems as providers of capital are better situated than countries at the periphery.[8]

The magnitude of the financial market is overwhelming, and when big crises occur, they can destabilize entire national economies. Such was the case in East Asia in the mid-1990s,[9] though its cause is often disputed. Soros holds that the financial weakness of South Korea, Indonesia, Malaysia, the Philippines, and Thailand was caused by internal political mistakes. According to many international politicians, the countries were disadvantaged in the international financial market.[10]

The "informal" market, which includes all those goods and services—such as household work—neither paid nor tallied in formal economic terms, has been of particular interest to women in economics. It is a factor crucial to the survival of many people, particularly women and the economically disadvantaged. Estimations of the size of the informal market are hard to obtain, but the 1995 Human Development Report offers a rough estimate: more than half of the gross domestic product of industrialized countries comes from this market.[11]

Other markets include black markets, trafficking in women, and drug trading.[12] All of these are illegal, but they also involve enormous amounts of money and are global in scope. Informal, and often criminal, markets exploit the very laborers who are unable to make a living within the formal economy.

Supply and Demand

What precisely happens in the market? In the traditional theory, free, well-informed people meet there to get the best deal possible for their goods and services and to maximize their utility. Activity in the market is mainly influenced by a demand side and a supply side of money, goods, services, and labor. The outcome of supply and demand in the market is the "right price."[13] In a perfectly competitive market, the right price will be established when both demand for and supply of any particular goods and services meet at an equilibrium.[14] "Equilibrium price" is the price at which the quantity demanded equals quantity supplied. Thus, if someone figures out a way to produce more of the same goods for a cheaper price, the demand for these goods will increase until the level of marginal utility (or incremental benefit from those goods) is reached at the lower price.

Consumer preference may also increase demand for some goods: this results in a higher price if there are insufficient supplies of those goods. New agents will then appear to produce the goods at a lower price as long as there is a profit to be made in doing so. At the point where there is no additional profit at a set price, production at that price will diminish.[15] On the other hand, there is a saturation point at which the consumer may not buy more goods because she has had enough. For example: the general Swede may indeed drink more coffee given a lower price, but even for Swedes there are limits to the amount of coffee they will drink! The marginal utility of coffee compared to other goods will reach a limit, and a lower price will only change that limit marginally.[16] Some other goods are very precious to Swedes, and they will limit coffee drinking when the price gets so high that they cannot buy more gasoline. If, for some reason, the goods increase in price, the demand will drop until a new price is fixed.[17] In other words, demand for coffee will increase until the price rises to a certain level, relative to the prices of other goods, or a saturation point is reached, after which demand will fall. The elasticity of such demand will vary, depending on how much the particular goods are seen as necessities or luxuries by the consumer.

People may also change their preferences for different commodities and hence increase or decrease their willingness to spend money on those commodities. If information, style, or desire for a particular commodity changes, people may well change their preference and choose to buy more of the same or something else. The variables that may figure in the dynamism of supply and demand are many-faceted and have always been under close observation and analysis by economists. The theory is that, given a free market, variables such as free movement in and out of the market and perfect competition will eventually produce the best possible utility or satisfaction or benefit for everyone and result in the right price.[18] This is the mechanism behind the work of "the invisible hand."[19]

Economic theory about supply and demand is well elaborated. It is a helpful theory that improves our understanding of what happens in the production and distribution of goods and services, and at what levels it occurs. The theory of supply and demand explains what happens in the market when the market works.[20] In theory, at least, the ideal market is a place where goods and services are exchanged without any need for supervision or regulation. In reality, however, there are no unregulated markets.

Scarcity

Scarcity refers to the fact that resources are insufficient to meet all the sorts of desires and wants of consumers indefinitely. Every, or almost every, consumer and household must choose its consumption of goods and services.[21] Lipsey writes: "For most of the world's 5.5 billion human beings, scarcity is real and ever present. In relation to desires (for more and better food, clothing, housing, schooling, entertainment, and so forth) existing resources are woefully inadequate; there are enough to produce only a small fraction of the goods and services that are wanted."[22]

Scarcity dictates whether producers have the wherewithal to supply the market and consumers have monetary or other resources with which to buy them. Where resources are scarce, there may be no market at all. For the producer of goods and services, it is necessary to find a market where there exist resources so that he or she can sell goods and continue production. The consumer needs resources to be a buyer in this market. Thus, it is only reasonable that markets with money and goods and services run better than markets with fewer or scarce resources. Most scholars recognize that extreme scarcity of necessities and resources is the reality for many people on this globe. The United Nations Development Program (UNDP) claims that the global economy has enough supplies of basic necessities to satisfy survival needs for the inhabitants on the globe, but they are not adequately distributed.[23]

At the 1995 United Nations World Summit for Social Development in Copenhagen, delegates from the international community agreed to a "20-20 policy." Nations in need of help would dedicate 20 percent of their total budgets to provide for basic education, basic health and nutrition, reproductive health and family planning, water, and sanitation; and donor countries would devote 20 percent of their aid budget for those services.[24] The total cost for those services to poor countries was estimated at $40 billion per year.[25] At this summit, governments took it upon themselves to eradicate poverty.[26] The global community, of which UNDP is a party, stresses the policy dimension of distribution of resources to provide for these needs. Many economists favor a situation where public policy allocates resources through public channels and political decisions so that everybody's basic needs are satisfied. In reality, the market is open only to those with purchasing power.

Again, are resources really scarce? It is true that not everyone could follow every whim every day. But it is not true that we have scarce supplies of food, water, air, money, labor, or less tangible necessities as love, intellectual capacity, and willing people. Some of those items are scarce in many places and at certain times, and figures showing the unequal distribution of access to monetary resources, for example, are striking. The poorest 20 percent of the world's population went from claiming 2.3 percent of the world's total income in 1960 to 1.1 percent in 1994. The richest 20 percent possessed 86 percent of the world's income in 1994.[27]

If there are enough resources, the remaining problem is one of distribution. For mainstream economic theory, this is simply not considered a problem. According to mainstream economic theory, if a need for distribution cannot be handled through the market mechanism because of insufficient resources of those in need, then that is a political rather than an economic problem.

"Economic Man"

The neoclassical economic assumption that people are well-informed, rational, and maximize their own utility implies a whole theory of the person—an anthropology—that we might call the economic "ideal person," or, more simply, "economic man." Much critique is focused on the economic man, and it is important to understand that this is not merely a theory of human psychology in economic theory but a model that actually functions in the marketplace.

Not every individual is well-informed, rational, and utility-maximizing, but this description provides a close enough (for mainstream economics) understanding of human behavior in general to offer a sufficient basis for theorizing. The reason for this sufficiency is the "law" of large numbers. What is explained or predicted in economics is not individual behavior but behavior of large numbers of people.[28] That humans act "rationally" in the economic arena is a fundamental assumption in economic theory. It is on the basis of rationality that people's preferences are developed in a self-interested and utility-maximizing manner. It is the rational human being who is looking to be well-informed. Of course, on both the rational and the well-informed score, people are fallible. However, many economists hold, humans behave rationally enough to provide the information needed to calculate human behavior and preferences. This conception of rationality assumes that preferences are organized to be exchangeable, and also predictably exchanged. Lipsey writes: "Rational expectations are not necessarily always correct; instead, the rational expectations hypothesis assumes that people make the best possible use of the available information, which implies that they will not continue to make persistent systemic errors in forming their expectations."[29] To be as rational as possible, perfect information is necessary, but it is not always obtainable. People are rational with the best information they can get. Or people are as rational as they can be with the information they have obtained and processed correctly. And that is enough for theorizing.

Still, to what does "rationality" refer? When rationality is raised as the cause of specific human behavior, it is common enough to assume that, in theory at least, rationality refers not to individual tastes and preferences but rather to a more generalized human capacity. In the case of neoclassical economics, generalization about large numbers tends to eliminate specific differences between individuals or among peoples. The correlation between large numbers and rationality seems to limit itself to the ability to make models and measure statistics. That is well and good, but of limited use in the prediction of human behavior. As critics of neoclassical economics argue, there are any number of other reasons for making decisions in the market: ideas about what is most important, tradition, status, moral principles, charity, feelings, or integrity in relation to other human beings and nature, to name a few.

Marginal Analysis

Much economic analysis probes not the static situation in which all the economic variables stand in equilibrium but how fluctuation or marginal change in any of them causes changes in the others. For any product or service, on the supply side, variables include the number of suppliers, availability and price of resources, access to the market, and, of course, offering price. On the demand or consumer side, they might include need, availability of substitutes, numbers of buyers, and tastes and preferences. Since incremental change in any of these variables can affect price, a crucial determinant for decisions about what and how much is produced is what happens at the "margin," or the "margin price." Producers will make or price commodities more cheaply or expensively, or produce them in larger or lesser quantities, depending on what is going on at the margin. For example, can one added dollar, worker, machine, hour, unit, or natural resource increase production or revenue or yield a higher profit—now, a little later, or much later? Or again, will closure of some marginal asset give higher profit? One worker, whose skills are becoming obsolete, may not be able to continue to produce more than he or she costs, and profit will increase if that person is fired. According to theory, the production of a commodity will cease when or slightly before the cost of production has reached the margin price at which it sells.[30]

Exogenous Facts, Externalities, and Collective Goods

Examples of collective goods are military defense, beacons, schools, roads, some utilities, mass-transit systems, and courts of law—necessary things that have not been profitable on the regular market and have hence become the responsibility of public institutions.[31] Collective needs tend to become the responsibility of the civil or political community since, because of their costs or scale, neither individual nor corporate citizens can fulfill those needs on an individual basis.

Collective needs are not provided for in many countries of the world, a fact that causes great suffering and disadvantages to the population. In those places, collective goods are considered "exogenous" to or outside the parameters of local markets since, lacking buyers with sufficient assets, they do not deliver a profit. Hence, they do not fit into conventional theory about the market.[32] Bits and pieces of those public systems have become privatized only insofar as they can be constructed in a manner that delivers a profit in a market. In this connection the "free-rider" problem occurs. All economic actors—suppliers and consumers, individuals and firms—benefit from collective and public goods (like air and water), the cost of which is not reflected in market prices. And what if people benefit from public goods but make a conscious choice not to contribute, after having weighed as negligible the risk of being caught? Or what if their economic activity causes environmental damage, and the cleanup costs are in effect shifted to later generations? Whether this is seen as a problem of private or political systems, or a problem of law-abiding citizens, or a problem of market failure, depends on different situations or contexts.

When it comes to the complex matters of the environment and non-renewable natural resources, market theory is facing new problems. The most important critique of economic theory's inability to consider public goods and "external costs" arises largely from environmental circles. Until recently, economic theory avoided the problem of environmental degradation by seeing it as an external cost, exogenous to the theory.[33]

Advanced Models

Economic theory tries to determine underlying causes and effects—often a complicated theoretical process. Even considering just a few variables can necessitate complicated analyses. Econometrics is a specialized branch of economics that utilizes mathematical abstractions and complex models of economic behavior. Many neoclassical economists prefer econometric analysis because its mathematical cast more closely resembles the conspicuously successful natural sciences than more cumbersome social-scientific methods.

While advanced economic models present important theoretical challenges and are clearly valid research methods, their findings are often not applicable to daily life. They are not used for prediction or to solve real problems, such as inequality, scarce resources, or the distribution of limited resources.

Emergence of Feminist Economics

Feminist economists set out to challenge the underlying assumptions, philosophies, ethical stances, and epistemologies of traditional economic models, especially as they affect women. In the most general sense, feminism has aimed to analyze the oppression of women based on biological sex or socially and culturally constructed gender roles and to find ways to end this oppression. Feminist economists take a hard look at crucial components of economic theory: objectivity, the economic "ideal person," rationality, rights, and equality.

Oppression of women is the oldest form of oppression still in existence, and perhaps we are now beginning to see a worldwide, broadly based effort to end it in every area of life, including economic life. Feminist economics is a rapidly growing field of research. The first burst of feminist research into neoclassical economic theory did not occur until the mid-

1980s and, as with almost all other feminist theory, it appeared first in the Western hemisphere. One important pioneer in the field was Danish economist Esther Boserup, whose work appeared in the 1970s.[34] Her specific field was developmental economics, and she has inspired many researchers active presently.[35]

Feminist economists are not a unified group; they come from many different perspectives.[36] Feminist work is also done in a variety of economic fields, conspicuously in developmental economics, such as in the work of Bina Agarwal and Gita Sen. Economists Nancy Folbre and Julie Nelson are significant contributors to the growing body of theory in feminist economics, and they have also contributed to major critiques of neoclassical economics.

Sex and Gender in Feminist Economics

The starting point of neoclassical economic theory is the empirical method.[37] Insofar as method begins with experience, feminism and economics share common ground. When feminist economists employ feminist economics, they analyze what is happening to women by using different variables directly tied to experience, such as wage differences, working hours, bargaining power, and leisure time, all as correlated to biological sex.

In addition to economic analysis, feminist economists also make contributions to theory about construction of gender, and they strive to see how gender and biological sex interact.[38] They use the concept of gender to expand our understanding of what is happening to women and men in the economic arena and also to expand the arena itself. Feminist economists are "standpoint" theoreticians because they argue that, seen from certain perspectives, women have experiences that have been neglected in economic theory and practice—and someone needs to speak from that standpoint.[39] For instance, women have insights and knowledge from work in the informal sector that is never translated into economic theory and rarely remunerated. Reasons for this standpoint are obvious: economic theory is inadequate when the perspective of over half of the world's population—women—is disregarded.

Feminist economists like Nelson argue that women and men, given the same education, experience, information, and values, do not differ in their ability to reason.[40] Yet she argues further that women are subject to different education, values, and facts—that is, they have different experiences than men.[41] To a large extent, this is true. In feminist economics, then, the whole discussion about standpoint theory is dealt with in a factual way. In a materialist worldview, differences come out of different social and economic locations, and those differences in turn result in different experiences and different perspectives on issues.

I think that it is important to insist on the distinction between biological sex and the construction of gender. Both have implications for feminist economics. It is safe to say that most statistics about women are not gender-specific. And, while other statistics do figure in biological sex, they do not always include a theoretical understanding of the construction of gender as it pertains to the specific area studied. Further, to deny that women's perspectives are sufficiently different to provide useful data for economics or any social science seems counterproductive. When data are analyzed a certain detachment is required; it cannot be enough to say that "a woman said it" to support a claim. Yet women bring different concerns, questions, and methods to their study, and their standpoint undeniably alerts them to certain data perhaps not otherwise adverted to.

Feminists Define Economics

Feminist economists challenge some mainstream approaches in economics. Frances R. Woolley suggests that "mainstream orthodox economics" or neoclassical economics can be characterized by the assumptions of methodological individualism: individuals are assumed to behave in a self-interested way, and "the analysis is built on the individual."[42] Focusing on a collective category (women), then, Woolley presents an alternative feminist agenda for economics: "(i) to document differences in the well-being of men and women; (ii) to advocate policies which will promote equity; and (iii) to conduct research free from androcentric bias."[43]

Some portions of Woolley's approach, such as her first directive, are within the reach of tools provided by economics. There are measurable differences in well-being that can be observed in wage differences, distribution of family income, and hours at work. Women work more than men, and earn less than men, and they are not compensated with a larger portion of leisure time.[44]

Woolley also recognizes that well-being is a larger concept than what is measured by differences in wages, leisure time, or health.[45] Feminist scholars use *equity* and *equality* interchangeably. Here evaluation of what is meant by equity and equality is better served by political philosophy and ethics.

The most common feminist critique of economic theory is not focused on how economics is defined but rather on what it is missing, especially its lack of consideration for "real-life" data.[46] From a feminist point of view, the lack of regard for women's experience, for women's roles in economic life, and for data regarding women leads to doubts about the validity of economics and its methods.[47] Until recently, the field has lacked tools and theories to acknowledge or analyze subjects like the informal sector or the role of altruism in economic life.[48] This kind of feminist critique is coming from within the paradigm of neoclassical economic theory as well as from outside of the paradigm.

Critique of the Economic Paradigm: Form and Content

A large part of the feminist critique against mainstream economics has focused on the form and content of economic research. Method is the stronghold of economic theory, and feminist critique is aimed at the core of how the methods are applied.

In *Feminist Economics,* Sandra Harding exposes the failure of objectivity in mainstream economic theory.[49] Her concern is that large segments of economics that involve women are not included in mainstream economic research or are treated with what she calls "weak objectivity."[50] Therefore, she argues, economics wrongly attributes to itself the status of a value-free and objective science.

Harding recognizes and analyzes the difficulties involved in talking about objectivity. Some people are frequently deemed less objective in their reasoning because they belong to certain categories: women, welfare recipients, blacks, Marxists, or environmentalists, for example. People in these categories are considered overly emotional and thus less rational.[51] Some methods are also seen as more objective than others. Statistics and scientific experiments, because they are highly formalized and impersonal, are assumed to be more objective and highly prized.

Alternatively, Harding and other feminist economists aim for what they call "strong objectivity."[52] In feminist theory, strong objectivity considers more variables and more complex variables than does a traditional, minimalist approach to economic theory. Gender is, of course, one aspect that must be included, but also consideration of systemic power structures and implicit patriarchal values. The reaction to feminist standpoint theory has been fierce. One reason for this vehemence is critics' assumption that a feminist standpoint theory necessarily implies a "gynocentric" position—one that posits essential differences between women and men. Gynocentrism is founded in an epistemological claim and a view of women and men as ontologically different. In economics, Deirdre McClosky represents such a position and in feminist philosophy Mary Daly is a prominent proponent.[53]

In fact, few feminist economists are gynocentric in their work. Still, the critics' underlying concern is one of utmost importance: how can we know about women's economic lives? The gynocentric position implies different epistemological claims from standpoint theory. Standpoint theory does not necessarily include a position that women and men have different abilities or ways of knowing depending on gender. The claim is rather that different perspectives provide different knowledge and that the knowledge women have gained from their different and particular perspectives is still widely though unwisely disregarded.

How does economics deal with real-life data? Since experience is so important to feminist economists, a certain amount of energy has gone into looking at this question. The long and the short of this endeavor is that data are hard to handle and that in order to make the theories work, "data mining" (cleaning out data that do not fit with main trends) is a recognized and accepted way of handling information in mainstream economics.[54] Two problems arise: why are real-life data not a sought-after source of information in economic theory, and why are data not treated better?

The Informal Economic Sector

Feminist economists recognize the importance of the informal sector. Within structures of intimacy, we have needs, wants, and desires that are satisfied, at best in companionship, friendship, love, and family—and at worst, through power over and against others. In these structures of the informal sector, no exchange of money takes place and no market is involved. Work there may be driven by love or, on the flip side, by oppression or any other factor that motivates women to provide a major portion of daily needs and services without getting paid.

The most important part of the informal sector is the survival of the human species. Babies are fundamental to human society. Babies are highly desired and valued, and they carry with them responsibility for care, upbringing, and education that is often mistakenly assumed to be and economically accounted as free of charge. Waged or wageable labor is not expected to be involved in raising babies; no money is supposed to change hands and no monetary reward or compensation is received. But in reality raising children requires many jobs in the informal sector, such as shopping, cleaning, cooking, child care, and other valuable and necessary services. It is called "reproductive work," and responsibility for it is most often delegated to women.

No natural law prescribes that women take on these kinds of responsibilities. It is just another incident of a construction of the distribution of work that disadvantages most women and gives advantages to men and women with excess resources. People with enough resources have always paid for many services—to have their children cared for, fed, and educated. Queen Victoria, the mother of many children, rarely wanted to see them until they were a few years old.[55]

Feminists have argued that marriage, in a sense, is a cheap way for men to have their personal services taken care of. They also analyze marriage as an economic reality—a place where exchanges of goods and services happen. A beautiful and well-dressed wife, for example, is something to show off and may enhance a man's career. Transactions within a marriage can also give the man access to sexual and other services,[56] while the woman, in turn, gets "security." In *The Dialectic of Sex,* Shulamith Firestone wrote:

> Now assuming that a woman does not lose sight of these fundamental factors of her condition when she loves, she will never be able to love gratuitously, but only in exchange for security:
> 1) the emotional security which, we have seen, she is justified in demanding.
> 2) the emotional identity which she should be able to find through work and recognition, but which she is denied—thus forcing her to seek her definition through a man.
> 3) the economic class security that, in this society, is attached to her ability to "hook" a man.[57]

This type of feminist analysis of economic implications of relationships between women and men has a long history and is still relevant in many cases. Such relationships are often driven by unregulated power. Market mechanisms are often operative in the informal sector where they are not infringed by political regulations. In most parts of the world, men control the scarce resources. An important feminist initiative has been to demand pay for work in the informal sector. If women were paid for this work, it would make the relationship between the sexes more equal. Due to pressure exerted by feminist economists, the value of the informal sector has at least received some recognition. Efforts are being made to estimate the value of the work in the informal sector. Newer estimates have shown that the informal sectors provide value that is comparable to the value of work and production in the formal sector. Sustenance of a large portion of the world's population is maintained in the informal sector. The food-gathering, fuel-gathering, cooking, gardening, and farming for the family that happens within the informal sector make the difference between life and death for the people involved. Yet all study of this sector happens outside mainstream economics.[58]

The Family

Until modern times the family was the common economic unit in society. Some claim that women fared better within this traditional framework, while others claim that women's lot was worse. Be that as it may, the economic status of the family has changed drastically, not only in the Western world but everywhere.[59]

"New Home Economics" is a popular theme in feminist economics. Even before the work of economist Gary Becker and his eloquent way of putting a price formula on every exchange that happens within the family, the topic was crucial for feminist economists. In mainstream economic theory, the family has been viewed as an unproblematic unit represented by the head of the household, a man, who has a separate existence as an individual in the market. In this way, analysis and valuation of the problematic transactions that happen within the family are avoided. The market is not connected to groups of people, a family, but to an individual, the male head of the household.[60] When a man appears with other men in the marketplace, he is fully his egoistic self, the "economic man." When he gets home, he takes off his coat and becomes the altruistic benefactor.[61]

The simplistic understanding of altruism in the family, as elaborated by Becker, is that being nice is a self-rewarding behavior: it's nice to be nice. Therefore, altruism is but another way to increase utility and is in no way contradictory to personal utility and pleasure.[62] Becker explicitly excludes the need for a philosophical interpretation of altruism: what is offered by economic theory suffices.[63]

But there are also cases in which the benefactor, who may be the main breadwinner of the house, chooses to take on pain on behalf of her or his dependents. This goes to show that altruism is a more involved and complex concept than can be explained by economic theory alone. Becker's counterargument then is that, if pain is self-inflicted and caused by a decision made by the benefactor for some not-so-obvious goal motivated by altruism, it may still increase that person's pleasure or utility. The problem tends to get out of hand when more people are involved in decision making. Who, then, decides whose utility or altruism determines the final decision?

When this difficulty is also overcome, all that is left is for the economists to construct the method and calculations accordingly. As Becker has taken (altruistic?) pains to show, there are ample opportunities to formalize these matters and make economic theory out of altruism. But important information is pushed aside, and this is where feminist economists have objected. Even conventional wisdom usually acknowledges women as the main distributor of altruism in the family, whereas Becker manages to put the male head of household in this position.[64]

Feminist economists, and feminists in general, have a more complex view of the family. Women's work in the family often is not something they choose or even have the option to change. In the family, the fact that historically men had all the power and made all the decisions was the basis for much conflict between husband and wife. How resources are allocated in the family is a well-known source of conflict, one that has a direct connection to differences in power.[65] The power differentials in families in which the man is the sole earner of cash are hard to ignore—at least by those who lack power.[66]

In 1990, half of the people in the United States who lived below the poverty line lived in households headed by women.[67] A majority of the fathers contributed little or nothing toward the support of their children.[68] Women in the United States generally earned 71 percent of the salary of males, if employed full-time.[69] In 1960, single mothers headed 7 percent of the families below the poverty line; by 1984 this figure had risen to 23 percent.[70] Single-parent households are regarded as a growing problem that makes women economically vulnerable. To help alleviate this phenomenon, feminists have urged that services—including child support, child care, education, equal wages, and affirmative action—be further extended so female heads of households may increase their earning capacity and decrease their dependence on welfare. Recognizing the complexities of family life and its needs, feminist economists work to expose the gaps created when the individual is the basic unit of measurement in economics. As commonsense as their work may seem, feminist economists still face strong resistance in their field. Responding to feminist essays collected in *Beyond Economic Man*, economist Robert M. Solow writes:

> It bothers me that the papers in this volume say almost nothing about the nuts and bolts of economic analysis; demand and supply elasticities, the cyclical behavior of real and nominal wages, you name it. The ideological content of economics attracts attention but were it not for the nuts and bolts, the market for economics would clear at a very low level. When it comes to the nuts and bolts, however, economics is more like chemistry.[71]

Dethroning the Market Model?

Neoclassical economics is a social science with far-reaching ambitions, trying out its methods on all kinds of social phenomena, even in Becker's "home economics." The more exact range of neoclassical economics—the range of areas in which traditional economic analysis can be fruitfully applied—is not so easy to define since there is no strong consensus on the matter among neoclassical economists themselves. Some prefer to keep a loose boundary and declare that whatever the method can do, the method can do. Others would prefer that economics keep a more orderly house and improve its methods before spreading them thin. Still others want to reconnect the tradition of moral philosophy and economics. Even so, most agree that the main focus of economics is the market in its many versions. As we have seen, to analyze markets, economists look primarily at supply and demand, the market mechanism, and the variables whose interplay determines the right price and market equilibrium.

Feminist economists and mainstream neoclassical economics differ in a number of important areas. The differences are mostly connected to the informal sector, the family, "economic man," and the lack of gender sensitivity prevalent in mainstream economic science. The absence of women both in the field of economics and in research within the science is also an issue. Most importantly, though, feminist economists critique the core of economic science: its concepts of objectivity and empiricism. In the next chapter we will see more specifically how two feminist economists address this crucial matter.

2

FEMINIST CRITIQUE OF OBJECTIVITY AND EMPIRICISM IN ECONOMIC THEORY

Feminist economic theory is fueled by its critique of mainstream economics. In this chapter I explore that critique, as well as why feminist economists use ethical concepts in their work. Five key concepts come into focus: gender, empiricism, objectivity, power, and basic human needs.

First, then, while the social construction of gender is a common theme in feminist theory, the actual construction of gender is complex. How do feminist economists contribute to the topic? Julie A. Nelson's and Nancy Folbre's critiques of neoclassical theory strike at its core: empiricism and objectivity. Second, money and power are interdependent in many ways. How do economists perceive the power and economics constellation? Third, from a grassroots perspective, the lack of basic human needs is a persistent problem throughout the world, and poverty is partially measured as lack of money. How do feminist economists address the fulfillment of basic human needs?

Gender in Feminist Economics

Feminist economists like Folbre and Nelson use "gender" as an analytical category to critique and improve neoclassical economic theory. But how do they understand gender?

The single most obviously gendered phenomenon in economic theory is the traditional concept of an "economic man." Folbre denounces the assumptions about human beings that are embodied in the traditional idea of the "Rational Economic Man," or Mr. REM. The assumptions behind Mr. REM—the rational, self-interested economic actor—ignore initial allocation of financial and human capital and the formative process that determines tastes and preferences, she argues. Folbre maintains that people do behave in truly altruistic ways that do not correspond with mainstream economic theory. People do engage in causes that serve their own interests, as classical theory asserts, but are motivated more by collective interests than individual self-interest.[1]

As feminists like Folbre point out, people do not in fact maximize their utility as economic theory contends. Further, no one has all the information needed to act in a completely rational manner. And no one is completely rational. Likewise, we are all affected, positively and negatively, by noneconomic factors, such as culture, class, and religion.

However, Folbre notes, neoclassical economics has changed some, more recently allowing for a new concept that is slightly different and less gendered than the traditional one in neoclassical economics. As Folbre characterizes it, the "Imperfectly Rational, Somewhat Economic Person" (IRSEP) has replaced Mr. REM in much of present economic theory. Because they see that the future is uncertain, information is expensive, and markets are imperfect, economists now show a growing willingness to reassess basic concepts of their field. Still, the IRSEP does not provide sufficient material to analyze the power relationship in economics, nor does this model resolve the issue of collective interests that still confounds traditional economics.[2]

The mainstream thinking that lies behind much of the construction of economic theory may have influenced the contemporary understanding of what constitutes a human being more than we know. How the classical model of self-interested, utility-maximizing persons affects and influences a contemporary person's notion of self is hard to establish, though several hypotheses along those lines have been tested.[3] Direct cause and effect are difficult to establish. If students of economics study individual maximization, for example, it is not necessarily a direct consequence of their studies: they may well have entered economics because they were utility maximizers to begin with. Overall, however, feminist economists find in the cultural legacy of economic anthropology a contraction of the notion of person, and specifically as gendered.

In her effort to conceptualize an understanding of gender, Nelson draws on the work of the linguists Georg Lakoff and Mark Johnson and feminist theologian Catherine Keller.[4] Nelson wants to find out in what way our notions of gender are constructed socially. She explores gender-related metaphors to add to our understanding of the economic contraction of our ideas of gender. Use of metaphor also helps enlarge the understanding of what it is we refer to when we think of feminine and masculine characteristics. In her view, construction of gender goes deeper than what is usually suggested by social construction theory: it also involves tradition, culture, and religion, which determine how we structure our very thinking and language.

Nelson is careful to term gender characteristics *feminine* and *masculine* instead of *female* and *male* to underscore her thesis that gendered characteristics are the basis for the difference, not biology. Nelson underscores that there are two genders and the two genders provide the basis for different treatment of women. One main feature is that gender is inherently connected to value.[5]

One gender has been central to economic theory all along: the masculine. This gender is taken as a given and implicitly assumed.[6] To accomplish the deconstruction of gender, Nelson looks at the dichotomies that are typical of gender, again avoiding biological sex as a distinguishing category.[7] One problem with her approach is that it can be interpreted as a concession to essential gender differences. She addresses biology and essentialism (the idea that biological differences between women and men entail very different modes of thinking and behaving) by rejecting a theory of extreme differences in nature between men and women.[8] But Nelson accepts the fact that some consequences follow from biological differences. For instance, to speak about marital abuse and disregard biological sex would be to hide the real situation of women.[9]

Nelson's Gender-Value Compass

Nelson shows how gender has been charged with metaphorical meaning that is derogatory to women as well as to men. There are traits attributed to the masculine gender that generally are conceived as negative, such as aggressiveness and shallowness in relationships. And there are feminine traits that are highly valued, such as sensitivity to others. Yet, feminist analyses have shown how traditional thinking about "men" and "women" has been dichotomized. Characteristics associated with men have been valued, while characteristics associated with women have been devalued. Through the concept of a "gender-value compass," Nelson exposes patterns of gendered thinking and shows how both genders contribute to human characteristics on many levels.[10] Her compass provides a creative, critical perspective on the two genders: both genders have positive characteristics, while other characteristics are negative for both genders. Her point is that the positive and negative characteristics are different for the feminine and the masculine gender.

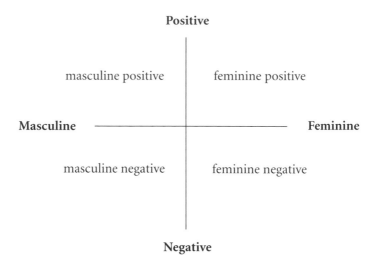

Figure 1

Nelson's gender-value compass is depicted by a cross-shaped diagram in which she places the socially constructed masculine on the left side and the feminine on the right side, and the positive above and the negative below the meridian (see Figure 1).[11] It enriches and deconstructs traditional ideas of gendered traits by finding both negative and positive aspects for both genders.

For example, being "scientific" is generally viewed as a positive masculine trait; the corresponding positive feminine trait would be "humanistic." A negative masculine trait would then be "inhuman" and the negative feminine trait "unscientific."[12] By tilting the usual approach to the construction of gender difference as expressed in hierarchies and dichotomies, Nelson's gender-value compass gives multiple options for understanding gender as a concept and how it plays out in multiple cultural venues. The biological differences are played down, while the construction of gender is opened up for a more complex understanding.

Empiricism and Feminist Economics

The role of empiricism in economic theory is a matter of intense debate among feminist economists.[13] Economic scholars are deeply involved with the construction of theoretical models of high complexity, and the level of sophistication in mathematics has made neoclassical economic theory a hallmark of scientific excellence. Yet much of economic theory is based on models and hypotheses that lack an empirical foundation. Many feminist economists expose such assumptions.[14]

For social sciences, of course, it is essential to take social data seriously. The task is to analyze and present information and to hypothesize about their meaning. So, the view that economics is a social science demands close attention to its social data. Both Folbre and Nelson view economics not only as a social science but as itself a social phenomenon, which means that culture, religion, politics, and many other factors contribute to the development of economic theories or systems, and that the science of economics is not just ontologically, or providentially, granted.

Nelson's critique of economic theory's lack of concern for social-science methodology is severe and stands in contrast to the frequent claim that economic theory is fundamentally based on method.[15] Too often, she asserts, economists work solely from models with little attention to actual data. She notes a lack of standard scientific method and laboratory work normally required of natural sciences. She refers to sloppy use of material and to "data mining"—a method researchers use to refine statistics continuously until they fit the theory. According to her, there is no merit in doctoral work in economics that does not include independent data gathering. Neoclassical economists often question the validity of the social sciences, partly for their inability to replicate earlier research.[16] Yet, this criticism often leads economists to depend too heavily on formal, rational methods instead of information gathered from actual social events. Nelson instead works for a more viable and complex theory geared to understanding social reality and to remedying social policy.[17]

Nancy Folbre arrives at the same criticism from a different angle. Folbre explores the political economy of the family, the nexus for caregiving work.[18] She uses neoclassical, Marxist, and institutional economic theory to position feminist political economy. Folbre could be classified as an "institutionalist economist" with a gender perspective. She looks at existing entities: structural factors (assets, rules, norms, preferences); agents (individuals, chosen groups, given groups); processes (coercion, production, exchange, coordination); and sites (firms, states, markets, families)—that is, real-life factors that provide data for theorizing.[19] Folbre's argument is that empirical data should draw on the experience of belonging to different groups and take into account various structural factors.

The failures of neoclassical economic theory to take actual economic data seriously weaken its scientific aspirations. The more proof that feminist economists provide about a deficiency in the actual work of neoclassical theory, the sooner it can improve. This kind of widespread and well-grounded discussion of neoclassical theory is now coming from environmentalists, development economics, sociology, Agenda 21 (an action plan from the UN environment meeting in Rio de Janiero in 1992), and, of course, feminist economists.[20]

Gender and Empiricism

Feminist economists are also concerned about how women are represented in economic theory. A main target for feminist critique has been how the informal and reproductive work of women has been disregarded.[21]

Is economics really measuring what it claims to measure? Marilyn Waring, a social scientist and politician, spent ten years investigating gender bias in the economic statistics and census data provided by the United Nations System of National Accounts (UNSNA). Much of UNSNA's work took place in order to implement the Bretton Wood instruments, the post–World War II agreements that framed the current international financial system. Waring reviews the work that redefined men's farm work as an asset and measured its value in money in order to include it into the UNSNA. She questions why it was deemed unnecessary or too difficult to measure the value of women's informal and reproductive work.

USNSA is a major source of information about national economies, and helps agencies decide which nations should be extended credit. Waring provided material for a radical consciousness-raising among feminists about economics through her analyses of what economists and statisticians did and did not measure.[22] To the UNSNA, a girl who spends the day collecting food and water contributes nothing to her country's gross domestic product (GDP). A well-educated man who watches screens in a top-secret, well-protected underground military facility, and whose input is at its best if he does nothing, has a high salary and a high value in his country's GDP.[23] Why? There is no exchange of money in the girl's work, but in the case of the well-educated man, there is money involved. In addition to finding the UN statistics badly lacking in accuracy regarding women's work, Waring found no statisticians willing to try to remedy the weakness of the figures.

The urge to raise consciousness about women's unaccounted work and to include women's work in GDPs has brought some results. Inclusion of women's informal work has been on the agenda of the women's movement all along, since the first UN Women's Conference in 1975, held in Mexico City. With more recent changes to the UNSNA system, accepted in 1993 by the European Union, International Monetary Fund, Organization for Economic Cooperation and Development, the UN, and the World Bank, the whole matter of the informal sector and intrahousehold services has been given new consideration.[24] The global community is now determined to include the informal sector in the UNSNA. One reason is that there has been a tremendous development of services that used to be provided in the household and that are now available on the market. Household services got a market price, and more devices were developed to estimate their value. Another reason is the realization of the size of the reproductive sector in economics.

In related research, the theory of supply and demand, equal pay for the same job, and access to waged work are discussed by Barbara R. Bergmann. She investigates to what extent the supply of labor is affected by wage demands. Women and minorities tend to receive lower pay for the same kind of work that men do for higher wages.[25] Why doesn't the demand and supply mechanism work in this instance? Why don't women and minorities get all the jobs if they cost less?

Bergmann elaborates on the theory of supply and demand, which maintains that market mechanisms decide the price of labor. The theory claims that demand for a certain kind of worker will decide the wage that an employer is willing to pay. In theory, at least, there can be no "wage discrimination" since the supply of workers able to do a certain job will decide how many skilled workers the employer will employ to meet demand. Then why are women and minorities paid less for the same work?[26] Bergmann's explanation for this contradiction is that what the employer is looking for is not only specific qualifications pertaining to the work, but other characteristics that will make the worker fit the job.[27] Significant characteristics are sex and ethnicity. If the sex is right—male—and the ethnicity is acceptable as well, the job is available and the wage is higher.[28] Inequity of labor and wages because of sex and ethnicity is easy enough to observe but hard to explain. Even when women and men are doing the same kind of job, the wages may differ vastly.[29] The supply and demand theory would then assume that the cheap labor would invade those jobs and increase the profit for the firm. Not so. And for this labor market failure, there is no explanation from within economic theory. Clearly the theory is inadequate to account for actual economic behavior. To find explanations for this conundrum, Bergmann turns to theories of discrimination.

Objectivity

The arguments and instances above raise questions about the scientific paradigm and objectivity of economics. Yet there is a place for mathematics, statistics, and constructed models in economics. Such models have made many useful projects possible.

For this reason, neoclassical economists have sometimes argued that economics should be seen and practiced as a natural rather than a social science.[30] Natural sciences look for inflexible, iron laws that guide and clarify what is happening in the arena of scientific endeavor. If economics is a natural science based on ontological truth, social data will be a low priority in the formation of theory. That is to say, if there exists an essence of economic science that can be revealed without access to social data, social data lose importance and do not necessarily add anything to the task of validating hypotheses.[31] However, I have not found any verification that would support claims that economics is a natural science harboring fixed truths that could be uncovered by research.

Feminist economists heavily critique the presumed objectivity of neoclassical economics. The kind of scientific aspirations that are a hallmark of neoclassical economic theory must, in their approach and results, pay careful attention to objectivity. It is at the heart of any scientific endeavor and is something that all scientists in all subjects regard as a trademark in their particular field. But objectivity is not easy to achieve, nor is it well defined. Johan Galtung explains the difficulties of achieving objectivity:

> If repeated observations of a constant phenomenon by the same observer yield constant data, the observation is said to be intrasubjective or reliable. If repeated observations of a constant phenomenon by different observers yield constant data, the observation is said to be intersubjective. These two requirements, reliability and intersubjectivity, can be used together as definitions of the loosely used term "objectivity."[32]

Reliability or intersubjectivity is required of empirical research so that the next person who carries out her research in the same manner is able to produce the same results. The next scientist must be able to test the results by repeating the procedure, to find out if a particular idea or result will be useful in supporting a hypothesis. Objectivity in this sense is necessary to exclude false or impertinent data from observations. This canon is elementary in both social and natural sciences.

Validation is also a basic component of scientific method, and it is achieved through repeating experiments or research.[33] Validity is achieved when research confirms strong correlations or cause-effect relationships through a method that is unbiased and with clear measures. Is the cause of the results we obtain what we assumed, or is there an underlying cause still undiscovered? To build knowledge and to formulate theory, it is necessary to be able to replicate previous investigations with the same measures as before.[34]

Aiming for objectivity in the methods and results of social sciences is highly complex, as pointed out by the Swedish philosopher Lars Bergström.[35] Does scientific objectivity demand that researchers distance themselves from values? It is neither possible nor desirable that scientists should be completely value-free. However, objectivity does require that consciousness of values be a part of scientific analyses and research designs so that biases in data collection or conclusions are avoided or at least accounted for. What motivates the researcher and her hypotheses when she designs her research must be separated from the presentation of the results, and this distinction requires attention.[36]

Are there other assumptions in objective research? Is the scientist biased—beyond personal motivations—by her research community and its traditions? Does the researcher need to be open and conscious about why she employs a certain method? Bergström reviews a number of such questions that press for objectivity in the scientific pursuit. He distinguishes between scientific research and scientific results in the areas he reviews, and he looks at the micro- and the macrolevels independently. He concludes that there are few and difficult means for determining objectivity, but he nevertheless advocates impartiality, value-free results, truth, completeness, and intrasubjective testability.[37]

Feminist scientific work has no objection to objectivity as such, only to the truncated and simplistic ideas of objectivity that inform much ordinary science. Many feminists note that objectivity is one of the areas where patriarchal science has failed by excluding information from women, ethnic groups, the poor, different cultures, and religions. Science has up until now been ignorant about "androcentric, Eurocentric, and bourgeois assumptions that have been virtually culture-wide across the culture of science."[38]

Women and oppressed men have perspectives and experiences that are disregarded, and they have a legitimate reason to demand attention and to have their observations included.[39] There has been a tradition of assumed objectivity by those in authoritative positions in science—those who have had the power to set the agenda for research and analysis. People in positions of power are particularly prone to bias in favor of people in their own circles. If a scientist is dependent on superiors for jobs, promotion, or approval, he or she may accept a perspective that is otherwise unconvincing.

Objectivity and Gender in Economic Scholarship

In her article "Can Feminist Thought Make Economics More Objective?" philosopher Sandra Harding reviews the critique of objectivity from scientist-philosopher Thomas Kuhn onward, emphasizing what feminist theory has revealed.[40] Her intention is not to abolish method and objectivity but to sharpen those tools by adding feminist insights.

A major addition to the understanding of objectivity in economic theory is the fact that economic community often is dependent on the work of women.[41] If this work is invisible when research is designed and conclusions drawn, we are faced with what is called a "weak form" of objectivity.

Relativism of knowledge is fairly well accepted in contemporary thought. Knowledge tends to be incomplete, for the simple reason that knowing everything is beyond human capacity. Knowledge about finite and limited objects can be impressive, but the finite object has proven often enough to be more complex than assumed. Facing this reality, scientists should work out the best theory possible at a given moment but also be prepared to change categories, paradigms, and perspectives if their theory is proven wrong. This kind of relativism is better described as having "encompassing" or "limited knowledge" of a certain object or activity.[42]

Epistemologically, economic science draws heavy fire from feminist economists. Why are so many relevant questions not asked? Why is so much information, and particularly the information that women can contribute, disregarded? This is one point where neoclassical theorists are losing credibility today, and the problem increases with their unwillingness to participate in dialogue with nontraditional groups. Instead, neoclassical economic science is holding on for dear life to its theoretical center: the assumptions of rationality, utility maximization, and adequate information.[43]

As discussed earlier, the Rational Economic Man (REM) has traditionally been the model for how humans behave in economic theory and practice. But, as Folbre has shown, the massive attack launched against Mr. REM in the last two decades has weakened this position.[44] Some economists are beginning to acknowledge the complexities of real-life situations, the complex development of human identity, and the constructions of gender, race, and family.

Nelson gives examples of the epistemological ideal of "detachment" as one basis for her critique of objectivity in economic theory. One form of detachment is to neglect the community that influences almost all of human activity.[45] It is in community that much of the caring work of women is done. Other forms of detachment are from the object of study and from other researchers. Many feminist scholars have worked in close contact with their research objects, which at times has provided them with new understanding.[46] By necessity, the acquisition of knowledge connects the researcher to others, if she believes that knowledge is a social construction, as opposed to a revelation. As practiced in contemporary economics, Nelson is arguing, misplaced ideals of detachment actually harm economic objectivity.

Nelson uses the gender-value compass to determine what is positive and negative in both the typically masculine and the feminine gender approaches to objectivity. She ascribes connectedness to the feminine gender in scientific problem solving and separation to the masculine gender. Faced with a particular research problem, the masculine gender, on the positive side, is concerned with understanding, while the feminine gender, on the positive side, is concerned with practical problems. On the negative side, the "separated masculine" gender is only concerned with abstractions, while the "connected feminine" gender is only concerned with "quick fixes."[47] With this approach, Nelson provides a more complex and gender-sensitive analysis of the practice of objectivity.[48] To establish the strength as well as the weakness of androcentric bias in research, as Nelson does here, is a positive development.

Extending this analysis, feminist economists note that "connected," practice-oriented research often is devalued within mainstream economics, while the more highly valued separated and abstract research lacks objectivity and is partial and subjective in its own way.

In sum, feminist critique of economic science and its objectivity is quite sweeping and basic. While Bergström problematizes objectivity on many scores, he floats over the basics of the trade—to use the best methods available while testing hypotheses, the need for reliability and validity in measuring—as if they are unproblematic and too self-evident to require comment.[49] Yet it is precisely here that Nelson critiques economic science. In her view, economists rarely check each other's data, pay little attention to the research methods in other social sciences, and distance themselves from the society they want to describe or make predictions about.[50]

Folbre's Imperfectly Rational, Somewhat Economical Person, which is a much more credible real-life model for a variety of different social relations, complicates more traditional approaches to economic theory.[51] Folbre points to the real complexity of economic reality and how, in her view, a fuller account of economic constraints provides a better vehicle to analyze power.[52] She critiques both neoclassical economic theory and Marxist economic theory, both of which she thinks make their task too simplistic. People are constrained in many ways, not just by markets or modes of production. For economic theory to improve its objectivity, she argues, this complexity needs to be included.

Of research designs that aim at a more adequate understanding of experience in the economic realm, Folbre's effort certainly looks very commendable. Folbre's critique creates a space where economic research can utilize its best tools for economic science, but on a microlevel: it aims for objectivity and is firmly rooted in empiricism.

Power

Hierarchies are a central theme in traditional analyses of the construction of gender: those who end up in positions of power are men, and women tend to submit to subservient positions. Power is so obviously at play in hierarchies, but to say that power is socially constructed does not sufficiently explain all the ways in which its variables are at work.

Nelson views power as a function in human community and as something that is also exercised in the family. She denounces the atomism of economic man.[53] She argues that people live either as responsible persons-in-relation or as dependent persons-in-relation: either dependent on someone's power or in a position to exercise power over dependents. In both cases, money is often an integral part of dependency or responsibility, in the form either of surplus money or of lack of money.[54]

According to neoclassical theory, an altruistic head of the household distributes wealth to dependents.[55] This is also a position of power: "If he doesn't care very much, they don't get very much," Nelson explains.[56] She provides an example of how power relations affect resource distribution in the family. Suppose a parent or man, who makes the decisions for the family, is thirsty and wants to buy something to drink. When he realizes that having a lemonade with his family will cost him for three, since his two children also want one each, he ponders the situation. If he takes a beer, which the children cannot have, it will only cost for one beer. His wife drinks neither lemonade nor beer. This hypothetical example behavior conveys how bargaining positions in the family are affected by the person who has the decision-making power and that this position is connected to control of money.[57]

To look at what determines a person's power, Folbre elaborates on constraints, that is, structures within which a person's power is defined. The budget constraints that are commonly used in neoclassical theory assume that people's decisions are determined by their monetary assets. But, in fact, assets are a much more complicated construction closely connected to power. To analyze power and to understand constraints, Folbre presents four variables that affect how people make choices in the market, in the family, and in voluntary associations: assets, norms, political rules, and preferences. Assets are time and money, rules are handed down through law, norms are part of the membership of groups, and preferences vary among people.[58] Consciousness about those constraints will affect how people conceive access to power, as well as their ability to act, to make decisions, and to speak their mind. They can compare power and combine constraints with the six "collectives": gender, age, sexual preferences, nation, race, and class.[59] With the help of these different structures of constraint, it is possible to have a better understanding of how an individual is situated in society and in relationship to others rather than as a separated self, and to see how this situation creates possibilities for choice and control.[60]

Folbre uses property rights as an example of a category that is not necessarily gendered in law but which, in practice, may have grave consequences for women's economic situation.[61] Women are often at a disadvantage when it comes to legal entitlements. When property changes occur, they can turn out to be unfavorable to women.[62] Folbre uses a rights vocabulary in relation to justice. In spite of different contexts and different fields of research, she notes, rights are treated as an unproblematic concept except for the fact that they are not always realized. Injustice takes on many different shapes and forms—socially, culturally, and legally— but, in fact, she argues, all forms of it result in diminishing women's rights and disempowering women.

Basic Human Needs in Feminist Economics

A further, telling criticism by feminist economists is of the lack of concern in economic theory about how to provide for basic needs.[63] As discussed in chapter 1, scarcity itself is not the problem: there are immense material resources available. What would it take to give all able and willing persons a chance to fulfill their basic human needs? Put another way, when viewed from the perspective of the poor, the global household is dysfunctional: it does not provide everyone with the means to obtain basic needs. Nelson points to the theoretical challenge at hand and proposes a solution:

> As a practical matter, I suggest that our discipline take as its organizational center the down-to-earth subject matter of how humans try to meet their needs for goods and services. Economics should be about how we arrange the provision of our sustenance. This core corresponds better to the common sense of the term "economics" (and to the etymological roots of the term in the Greek words meaning "household management") than does the present central concept of the idealized market. This definition dethrones choice, scarcity, and rationality as central concepts.[64]

Here, Nelson boldly requests a new approach to and criterion for economic theory and practice. She develops a normative stance, using basic human needs as a criterion. Nelson writes: "Economics is sorely in need of a new system of values if it is to be able to generate more reliable, more scientific and objective (in the 'strong' sense) knowledge."[65]

Nelson places herself in the philosophical-ethical strand of economists when she asks for major rethinking within economics both on the grounds of the inadequacy of traditional ethics and on the grounds of a malfunctioning economic system. "Economics should be about how we live in our house the world," she insists, suggesting a more practical approach to economics.[66] Thoughtful proposals from mainstream economic theory would not successfully open up the present economic system to the poor, she argues, because theories do not work unless put into practice. Folbre and Nelson share an empirically based approach to their science and situate their work with real people and real problems in community, in particular the situation of women and children. Improving economic science to lighten the burdens for women and poor people are major aspirations.

Reconnecting Objectivity and Justice

Feminist economists' critique of neoclassical economic theory is over-whelming.[67] They are not aiming at some minuscule and marginal concern but rather at the heart of economic science—its methods and its premises. The critique is bolstered by data concerning gender, as gathered from the social sciences. As with many other feminist theoreticians, Nelson and Fol-bre accomplish their critique by complicating the theory and exposing social constructions and theoretical exclusions.

Nelson constructs her own tool, the gender-value compass, to show how values are crucial to economic science, that there are two genders, and that there are positive as well as negative characteristics associated with both the feminine and the masculine genders. She is explicit in her demand that economics focus on fulfillment of basic human needs.

Folbre shows how collectives—gender, age, race, etc.—and other con-straints influence the choices people make or don't make. Her description of how to understand what guides choices is sensitive to the experience of many women and provides a richer, more complex picture than simplistic economic models. She pays particular attention to rationality and points out the difficulties inherent in that assumption. Both Folbre and Nelson use ethical language to strengthen the case for a more contextual, gender-sensitive, and materialist economic science—which can be interpreted as a concern for justice.

Objectivity is a complex scientific criterion that embodies the highest scientific ideals. According to these feminist economists, scientific method should be intersubjective, verifiable, impartial, and coherent on the microlevel. It is the task of science to do its best with the intellectual resources at hand, considering existing values, ideologies, and results.

Yet feminist economists do not argue for a "detached," value-free sci-ence. For them, the questions that a scientist chooses to study are preferably based in her values or ideology, which will make the whole investigation more relevant and rich. New arguments will present themselves in the process and demand to be accounted for—and they should be. In this model, objectivity has no ontological grounding, but rather is a scientific construct that changes as our analyses, our methods, and our understand-ing improve. If "stronger" objectivity is a goal, and there seems to be a unan-imous conviction from feminists that it is, the critique that comes from people of other perspectives, different experiences, the poor, the marginal-ized, women, ethnic groups, and women from the South is essential for research design. Folbre, for example, calls for an interdisciplinary approach to economic research that will put children in focus.[68] Folbre is outspoken about a theory of economic justice in her alliances with feminist, Marxist, and neoclassical economic theory. Her objective is to achieve a democratic method by which to solve common economic concerns.[69]

It is at this point, where objectivity meets justice, that deeper questions of power arise. Power and money are closely connected. Monetary assets are unequally distributed between the sexes, and this is indicative of a power imbalance. Though still only obscurely understood, power is as crucial in economics as it is in all other forms of social relations—a point that the feminist movement in all its different modes has broadly uncovered. The common repressive instrument to sustain power is violence, while the major incentive is access to resources. In the next chapter, we examine its concrete operation.

3

EQUALITY, RIGHTS, POWER, AND BASIC HUMAN NEEDS IN FEMINIST DEVELOPMENT ECONOMICS

In this chapter I investigate how feminist economists use ethical norms to support their claims about rights, equality, power, and basic human needs.[1] Do they argue for any particular norms to govern economics? If so, are the norms implicit and assumed, or explicit and defended? To get at these concerns, I analyze the work of two feminist economists, Bina Agarwal and Gita Sen, who work primarily in development economics.

Feminist Economists and Equality

Bina Agarwal has surveyed a very great number of unpublished studies and scholarly work in anthropology and other social sciences about the situation of women in South Asia to substantiate her thesis about the relationship between gender and land rights for rural women.[2]

Her hypothesis is that the lack of actual ownership and control of land or its products leaves women in a much worse position in regard to all other economic activity and that this is a crucial determining factor in women's welfare, empowerment, efficiency, and equality. Agarwal argues that "women's struggle for their legitimate share in landed property can prove to be the single most critical entry point for women's empowerment in South Asia; and it seeks to bring this issue out of the wings onto centre stage."[3]

The strongest argument for equality in Agarwal's work is that equality is a sign of a just society. In her native country, India, the 1950 Constitution promises equality before the law, regardless of religion, race, caste, sex, or place of birth.[4] Justice thus becomes the larger context of economics, and for justice to be realized there must be equality. When women enjoy land rights, intergender relationships change in their favor and they gain greater levels of economic equality. Therefore, she argues, women should have the same land rights as men. Clearly, the notion of equality is important in Agarwal's work. But what does it mean when Agarwal assumes equality as a common and established value?

The Bodhgaya struggle of 1978–82 in the Gaya district of Bihar, India, against the Hindu Math monastery-cum-temple complex provides material for Agarwal to dissect several important issues for women's equality. This struggle over land was led by Vahini, a Gandhi-socialist youth organization that was formed expressly to struggle for land for the poor people that lived on the land and cultivated the land controlled by the Math. Women were involved along with men throughout this struggle and were also victimized when the Math terrorized them during demonstrations and strikes they initiated. When the issue of land distribution emerged, women demanded individually owned land and separate title to land. Only two villages wanted to give land to women. The Bodhgaya struggle was the first instance in which women were given the title to land in a variety of ways, although not on equal footing with men.

This distribution of land did not happen without discussion. Agarwal writes:

> The peasant male activists argued: "What difference does it make in whose name the land is registered?" The women responded; "If it doesn't make a difference, then put it down in the woman's name. Why argue over it? And secondly, if it makes no difference who owns the land, then why not let it continue to be owned by the Math?". . . . Equality can only strengthen, not weaken, an organization, but if it does weaken our unity, that will mean that our real commitment is not to equality or justice but to transfer of power, both economic and social, from the hands of one set of men to the hands of another set of men.[5]

Women wanted equality and, in order to achieve equality, the right to own land seemed basic to them. Even though it is not a sufficient right, in the philosophical sense, it is a necessary one.

Gita Sen and Caren Grown represent a network of women scholars in many disciplines from developing countries; it is called Development Alternatives for Women in a New Era (DAWN).[6] Sen and Grown do not focus specifically on equality but describe inequality in practice. They assert their understanding of feminism as a multifaceted enterprise with many different perspectives, united in a struggle against all forms of oppression based on gender and hierarchy.[7] They make a strong case for reconstructing the whole social fabric in response to oppression of people, and especially women, on grounds of race, class, and nationality.

To understand the nature of this oppression, they start with the most oppressed population: women. Women make up a majority of the poor, the underemployed, and the socially and economically deprived.[8] Women's work in the informal sector contributes to basic survival but is not accounted for.[9] In 1985, at the conclusion of what is referred to as the "first decade for women" because of United Nations attention to and consciousness of women's issues, it was almost universally conceded that the situation for the poor women of the world had in fact worsened during that period.[10] What Sen and her organization, DAWN, seek is an economic and social system that provides for basic needs.[11]

The success of development programs depends on how directly the people affected by the development are involved in the programs and the extent to which the programs are aimed at meeting basic needs. Sen and DAWN stress the importance of direct participation by the women themselves. They repeat this over and over again: there can be no good development if people come from above or from other areas to tell the local population how they will, can, or should manage a better economy. For development to take place, there must be local involvement and, of course, the involvement of women in all stages of the programs: the planning, the implementation, and the evaluation. The aim of development programs must be very clear: all efforts must point to the shortest way possible to solve problems of basic needs, including social, monetary, and employment policies. This requires inclusion of all people, both female and male, for whom the programs are devised. Hierarchical organizations that are insensitive to the community they are supposed to serve perform inefficiently, Sen implies. It is impossible, or at least very hard, for the elite to know about the needs of poor people. A proper understanding of the context of poor people requires dialogue with them to determine what their basic needs are and how they would want to carry out changes to provide for their needs. If poor people are not involved in the development process, instead of becoming self-reliant, they will become dependent on benefactors. Further, efforts and aims that are not presented and discussed with the people may be misguided and even counterproductive.[12]

Sen more explicitly identifies the problem of gender equality in her review of development programs. Since the programs tend to be gender-blind in themselves, it is hard to evaluate their effect on women's work, power, and autonomy, as well as how they affect the situation of the poor in a more general sense.[13] Sen states that even though both the World Bank and the International Monetary Fund have great influence on how development projects are designed, reducing inequality in asset holding has not been their major focus.[14]

Women's Rights in Theory and Practice

One of the main objectives in Agarwal's work is to show how women are discriminated against in land rights, specifically rights to own title to land, to control land, and to have usufruct over land. These rights have different origins. Some are related to a lack of legal rights to land; some concern the cultural rights to land; and some relate to customary rights to land. When Agarwal argues for women's right to land, she refers to this whole variety of rights—title, usufruct, and control of land—almost as if there existed a universal understanding of rights. She assumes that if women's rights were respected, women would own, control, and cultivate land on their own.

The specific rights Agarwal would like to have upheld are legal rights to claim property, which should be fully enforced by the judicial system if and when they are violated. She also suggests that women's rights to claim property should be upheld by religious or cultural communities. When Agarwal refers to women's rights, her basic understanding of rights concerns legal rights that can be claimed within the legal, cultural, or religious system. She notes that while it is often possible to find the framework for upholding legal rights, most often women's rights are violated anyway, and women have no recourse. There are no courts of appeal that effectively protect women's rights, even as they are spelled out in inheritance laws.[15]

Among religious groups, women are given smaller shares in land than are men. There are legal restrictions to women's entitlement to land in such places as Nepal and Sri Lanka. There are also legal restrictions on women's rights to dispose of their inherited land. There are "customary" restrictions on women's rights in land. Women's rights are often limited to usufruct, especially in the tribal communities in the northeastern states of India.[16] Also in India, women have inheritance rights that are equal to men's according to state law.[17]

There are, however, many ways to render those rights meaningless. Civil law distinguishes between different religious laws and secular law. Another route to rid women of their rights is the way local customs render laws invalid and force women to give up their legal claims.[18] Marriage customs are a particularly effective route to make women relinquish their legal rights. Yet another way is to harass women not to exert their rights. Agarwal gives examples of how women are denied the right to inherit paternal land and are threatened with losing potential economic and social support from brothers who also control potential access to the larger social arena.[19]

In some parts of South Asia, like Kerala, Sri Lanka, and northeast India, matrilineal inheritance laws and customs have given women title to land.[20] While this may sound positive, Agarwal makes some important observations about matrilineal practices and how they affect women. One characteristic of those practices is a tight control of kinship: women often marry second cousins. Although women stay on their native land in matrilineal cultures, whereas in patrilineal parts they move to their husband's family's land, Agarwal has found that women who own land in matrilineal cultures do not actually always control the land. Women often do most of the work on the land but are not in charge of either the cultivation or the land's products. Seldom do women in practice exercise the same marital rights in land as men.[21]

Land is the base from which much else develops. Ownership of land is a central issue for women's ability to create livelihoods on their own. Access to salaried work is heavily influenced by ownership, usufruct, or control of land. Women who own land have a much better economic situation, even if their property is small. The symbolic function of the ownership of land makes it much easier to find other sources of income. Agarwal points to an important internal relationship between land rights, gender, and such measures of well-being as basic welfare, efficiency, equality, and empowerment. The first, the welfare of women and girls, is dependent on women's ability to provide basic needs for their families. Women also spend more of their resources on the family than do men: 90 to 100 percent, compared to men's 75 percent.[22] Children's access to food has a much higher positive correlation with the income of the mother than with the income of the father. Also, the absolute poverty of families is related to ownership of some land. If they have access to land, they manage extreme hardships better and can still provide for basic needs.

But women's welfare cannot be established only by the economic status of the family. In cases of widowhood, divorce, or separation, women become more economically vulnerable. Widows of wealthy men may find themselves working in the fields of the land owned by their dead husbands, now in the hands of his family, at whose mercy she exists. Agarwal makes a case for common access and usufruct of land for groups of women by citing the success of the "Village Commons" (communal land, owned by a village), which has provided the landless with ways to feed cattle.[23] There has been a dramatic decline of these commons during the last few decades, which has made poverty worse.

Efficiency is the second basis on which to argue for women's land rights. Agarwal argues that if women own even small plots of land, they will use their land more efficiently than do men. She admits that it may be difficult to show that women are more efficient than men in economic terms, but she provides examples of how women's land rights would improve production on the land. And, she argues, if there were more small farms, which would be the outcome if women inherited land the same way men do, output would increase: "The existing evidence suggests that land redistribution from big to small farmers would probably increase agricultural output."[24]

An example of efficiency comes from the Grameen Bank in Bangladesh, which provides microloans to poor women.[25] Women who take loans use their money carefully and they are usually better credit risks. Agarwal also cites the "Chipko movement," which since 1973 has organized women to protect local forests, one example of how women care for the environment because they depend on it.[26] Inversely, distribution of work often leaves women responsible for collecting fuel and fodder for cattle, which may be very far away if the men decide to grow fruit trees for cash in the neighboring fields.

Agarwal is careful not to be trapped into arguing that biological differences cause cultural differences between men and women.[27] Hence, she sees the division of labor as the explanation for the women's intervention on behalf of the environment in the case above. For the women concerned, it is not efficient to spend half a day gathering fuel and fodder.

Although there are clear assumptions about rights in Agarwal's work, there is no explicit understanding of different kinds of rights, such as claim rights and "negative rights and positive rights," or of how rights are justified—though these are a basis for ethical theory. Thus, as an economist, she has not developed a thorough ethical theory.

Sen and Grown view women's rights from a perspective of reproduction. She maintains that in developing nations, women's reproductive rights are denied. There are many implications of women's lack of control of fertility, such as unpaid work in the household, child mortality, reproductive health, forced sterilization, and decreased access to the labor market, as well as an increasing number of people living in extreme poverty. Women's rights to their bodies are proclaimed in many versions. Reproductive rights preserve health, nutrition, family planning, autonomy, and economic options. As Sen and Grown argue, those who control reproductive rights are in a position of power in regard to women's bodies and lives.[28]

Reflections

Agarwal and Sen and Grown both pay substantial attention to issues of equality. Yet they treat equality as a norm that they take for granted, as if there is no need to argue for or against equality. In their economic research, they use the term *equality* without definition or explanation. They often refer to equality in the negative—that is, they point to *in*equality between women and men as a persistent pattern in economic practice and theory and how this inequality affects women. As a consequence, they tend to get stuck in circular arguments; if there is equality, equality will be improved.

Sen and Grown do not argue from an *ethical position* as to why women in oppressed situations should be involved in development on equal footing with all others. But their case studies of local involvement in development relate well to one important ingredient in *feminist theory* and practice: full and equal participation of the people concerned throughout the whole project and in the evaluation of the project.

Sensitivity to context is a crucial element at every step of development work as well as economic change. But it seems that Sen and Grown are content to say that consideration of equality is key in each and every project. There are no indications that some situations would be too peculiar to comply. Equality is a norm for which they argue fervently, as if this norm were recognized universally. Sen's analysis relies on equality as an assumed, normative objective, although the normative point is not articulated per se. In her work, the fact of inequality demands equality, but she provides no other argument to substantiate the demand.

Neither Agarwal nor Sen uses *equality* differently from how it is commonly used in Western feminist contexts, which in turn comes from the liberal tradition: equals shall be treated equally; each person has a vote and none has more than one. The authors' demands pertain mainly to equal legal rights and equality in regard to title of land, control of land, access to products of land, involvement in development, and shares of scarce resources. All these forms of equalities affect women's material and economic resources and are hence of importance to economic research. But, in their work, the underlying assumptions and arguments about equality are not spelled out. Neither Agarwal nor the DAWN collective are specific in showing how their understanding of equality relates to class, race, or religion. Their understanding of equality is that it should be a criterion used in all forms of economic practice and in economic theory. This criterion is simply an addition to economic theory and the practice of feminist economists. In fact, contemporary economic theory is at best only remotely concerned with equality, and in a roundabout way: if we are supposed to be rational, it is fair to assume that this would demand some kind of equal rationality. Economic theory does not consider if rational capacity differs between women and men.

Neither Agarwal nor Sen and Grown are primarily concerned with economic *theory* and fundamental changes to it. They start from the empirical fact that major changes, maybe even a change of paradigm in the market economy and change of focus in theory, have to happen in order for women to gain equality. To affect the real situation of real women is not a theoretical problem; rather, concrete actions to change their situation are needed. This echoes what Daly and Cobb argue in *For the Common Good:* theoretical constructions get in the way of real problems, and reality becomes a corrective to theoretical construction. The faults of economic theory, which they summarize as the "fallacy of misplaced concreteness," can be exposed by using empiricism, in this case findings from social sciences.[29]

Rights language figures prominently in feminist calls for equality. For instance, Agarwal demonstrates that women's rights are violated, and the result is inequity. Women do not have equal rights with men, nor do they have equal opportunity to claim their rights. In her reasoning, rights are best understood if subsumed under the ideal of equality. If women were to have equal rights with men, their economic situation would be changed drastically for the better. That is to say, rights should be distributed equally to women and men.

Power

The issue of power has been central to the women's movement since its inception.[30] Early feminism distinguished between "good power" and "oppressive power." "Oppressive power" is defined as the domination over and against others. "Good power" is power with and for others, empowerment, liberating power. Not surprisingly, the first kind is patriarchal power, and the other is power instrumental for liberation of the oppressed.[31]

One argument for equality is that equal rights to land empowers women.[32] In addition to the lack of legal title rights, Bina Agarwal also addresses the issue of control of land. When women own land, it may indeed be a mere formal ownership if women are not in control of land and its products. Then women only have a formal right with no practical implications.[33]

Control of land is a perfect locus for a discussion about power. Were women to have land rights, this would also give them access to political power. Support from other women would make it possible to participate in decision-making bodies.[34] To improve women's domestic situation, it is exceedingly important that they have their own means for survival—above all, the option to own land. This means power to define their own needs, speak their own minds, and not be dependent on husbands for survival.

Agarwal takes as a given that the transfer of power to women should be normative, that women should have equal power to men is a right. Why this is right and good is implicit in her work. For women, and particularly poor women, control is necessary in order to obtain any kind of power to change their situation. Agarwal defines empowerment as "a process that enhances the ability of disadvantaged ('powerless') individuals or groups to challenge and change (in their favor) existing power relationships that place them in subordinate economic, social, and political positions."[35] The issue of power gives direction to Agarwal's research and provides important research subjects related to women's economic autonomy and rights. Power in the household is one of the areas that has received close attention among feminist economists. They note that the breadwinner of the household has a natural upper hand in decision making.

In an essay in *Feminist Economics,* Agarwal investigates the different bargaining positions that are subsumed within a household to find out how they are constructed.[36] The power dynamics in the household are analyzed with emphasis on access to resources. Agarwal makes her case by analyzing how women are dependent on economic resources to defend their bargaining position—and often end up with the short end of the stick. Agarwal and other feminist economists argue with the traditional notion that households are unified economic entities governed by a single altruistic head of the household.[37] The point of her analysis is to see who has power to decide, and she defines her work as "analytical description."[38] Within this view, she argues that a formal model could be developed that would incorporate empirical analysis to see how gender is socially constructed inside the household. A multitude of variables affects a person's bargaining power within the household. Earned income is the one most recognized and discussed, but Agarwal adds other resources: arable land, earlier success in bargaining situations, position in the family, and participation in other decisions in the family.[39]

Social norms do play a part in the practice of bargaining, and it is a subject for close scrutiny. A particularly blatant example of this is the purdah tradition in some parts of the Muslim culture, which requires that all women wear a purdah, or veil. The demand that women live within this tradition limits their ability to take part in social and political organizations or do paid work. In Bangladesh, the Bangladesh Rural Advancement Committee (BRAC) has argued that the norms of purdah are constructed by the elite and used to keep poor women from advancing in society. When women do get involved and find better positions within the workplace and get a better grasp on economic issues, their position in the family improves.[40]

Agarwal raises the question of power: "If power is not to be seen as a thing in itself, we do need to ask: of what is this power constituted, and what is its source?"[41] Agarwal does not answer her own question but stresses the need to consider social norms for our understanding of what happens in intrahousehold bargaining.

For Sen, power connects to the issues of women, poverty, and development. Poverty is a growing problem for women and for women-headed households. Little money goes to women's development projects (when statistics discerning biological sex are available); women lack the necessary power to sustain their livelihood and to effect change.[42]

Sen and Grown analyze the costs and consequences of militarism at length, especially its devastating and useless waste of resources, such as money. Military spending was, and is, a growing stumbling block for developing economies. The money that goes to the military takes away resources that could be made available for development.[43] The connection between disarmament and development was established through the Special Sessions on Disarmament held by the UN on several occasions.[44] This connection was, of course, not left undisputed: at one of the sessions in 1988, in an infamous speech given by Danish representative Uffe Elleman-Jensen, the European Community denied that such a connection could be established.

As a way of changing the course of development, empowerment of women is a necessity. Poor women are central to this organizing and empowerment effort since they have the most to gain and the least to lose. To organize women requires resources of many kinds—some are financial; other just require know-how; and others require leadership training in democratic processes.[45]

Sen and Grown point to microloans and other initiatives that are specifically aimed at poor women as important steps for women's development.[46] They stress the role played by nongovernmental organizations (NGOs) in preparing grassroots initiatives in places like South Asia. NGOs tend to have a conscious strategy to empower women. For instance, DAWN is multifaceted and open to many different kinds of organizations, strategies, and objectives, with the main focus directed toward development opportunities for poor women.

Both Agarwal and Sen and Grown emphasize the connection between equality and power. Equality is a prerequisite for women's empowerment. Equality is necessary in order for women to be able to influence their situation on the same terms as everyone else. Equality would also give women access to the same resources as everyone else. Strict economic reasoning about power gives the impression that power and empowerment now are universally accepted concepts in feminist economics, and they are understood the same way everywhere. Power should be distributed among women and men in an equal manner.

Basic Human Needs in Feminist Economics

Sen and Grown stress the importance of *basic human needs*. They point out that a growing portion of the world's population finds it difficult to provide for basic needs. This has become a focus for many international agencies. The World Bank is also paying much attention to this matter, although the Structural Adjustment Programs of the World Bank have been deemed counterproductive to development for the poor.[47]

Since the "trickle-down" policies for economic development after World War II failed to deliver substantial new development in the Third World, a new strategy had to be found. The International Labor Organization (ILO) started in the mid-1970s to emphasize meeting "basic human needs" as a new strategy for development projects. For the ILO, basic human needs include food, health, water, sanitation, housing, and education.[48]

Today, the estimated number of undernourished people in the world ranges between 800 million and 1.5 billion. World Bank research estimates that 40 percent of the people who "survive" on less than a dollar a day live in India.[49] Poverty is much more severe among women compared to men in India.[50] DAWN´s critique of development programs is aimed at their gender blindness and oppression but also emphasizes that there is not enough concern about the lack of sufficient provision for basic needs.[51]

Agarwal looks at the situation of women who are laboring to provide for basic human needs. She centers her work in a materialist approach to economic reality and analyzes the detrimental consequences for poor women and even for more well-to-do women. She makes it clear that for women to have a dignified existence in South Asia, it is imperative that they have the right to own and control both the land and the products of that land. This is how Agarwal views the possibilities for women to provide for basic human needs, while Sen holds a more traditional feminist vision for how those needs can be fulfilled.

The Feminist Economic Challenge

Thus far, I have analyzed the work of four feminist economists to find how ethical concepts are used and have asked whether they are explicit and argued for, or if they are implicit and taken for granted.

As different as their contexts are, we have unearthed some fundamental similarities. First, gender is a category the authors use when analyzing economic problems relating to biological sex. The sophistication in the use of the concept of gender varies significantly. How women fare in the economic arena is to a large extent dependent on the construction of the feminine gender. But also the masculine gender, constructed as superior in most areas, excluding reproduction, is an important category. As discussed in chapter 2, Julie A. Nelson explores and deconstructs the construal of the two genders through her gender-value compass. The compass exposes the common strengths and shortcomings of both genders. Second, a common feminist focus is what happens to women in the economic arena, and particularly to poor women. They ask: can economic science or development economics or the market empower women, in particular poor women, to provide for themselves or to have their work valued in the same manner as men's work is valued? Their work vindicates the use of biological sex as a valid category in economic analysis.

Third is the issue of economic *objectivity*. Nancy Folbre and Julie Nelson aspire to improve economic science. They propose that this can be done with a better use of empirical knowledge. Economic scholars in the neoclassical tradition tend to neglect real data and problems in favor of constructed models. To remedy this, Nelson suggests improved research training in economics that would include social sciences and methods to confirm or validate results. Folbre shows that not understanding the complexity of basic conceptual constraints makes economic science noncredible in describing actual constraints. Folbre's critique can be subsumed within the concept of *thick objectivity* developed in feminist theory. To include in one's analysis all the complex variables that comprise the social construction of viable economic concepts is to adhere to thick objectivity. Thick objectivity requires that acquisition of knowledge in economic science be as complex as the rich processes it proposes to describe or predict.

Folbre and Nelson aim to improve economic theory, not to do away with theory. They want it strengthened, with the expectation that theory would improve understanding of people's hardships through acknowledgment of economic constraints, lack of objectivity, and ignorance of basic needs. While they are concerned about the lack of value orientation in economic theory, and while claiming a feminist perspective, they do not explicitly discuss justice as an economic norm. Value assumptions about equality, justice, and rights are implicit and taken for granted.

Fourth, feminist economics highlights the fact that *the informal sector* and *reproduction* are usually neglected in economic theory. In these areas, women carry a tremendous workload that is only now being valued monetarily.[52] It is well documented that most of the money that women in poor families earn goes toward the family, to a much greater extent than when men distribute their earnings. Yet mainstream economists have approached women's position in the reproductive and informal sectors with reluctance. In contrast, Folbre makes the point that this sector is crucial to human survival and should be recognized for a better understanding of the constraints that women face.

Fifth, *power* is a key issue in any feminist analysis and in all the texts reviewed here. The lack of resources for poor women also means a lack of power. Those in positions with power over others are easily recognized by the fact that they control and have access to resources. Resources give power to control, reward, and punish others. Agarwal and Sen, like Nelson and Folbre, take a materialist approach to their science and situate their work with real people and real problems. They look at consequences for women in real life as an important indicator for their work, and they pay less homage to abstract work and methods. The global household is in dire need of good, practical advice, they say, especially for those who live in situations of severe economic hardship.

Sixth are *rights* and *equality*. Both Agarwal and Sen and Grown assume that legal rights should be given to women and men on equal terms and in equal proportions. This assumption is explicit in their writing, but they do not explore different conditions of equality. There are different ways to interpret their silence on what constitutes rights. Their treatment of rights gives the impression that justice is a universally accepted concept and does not need to be explained. From this acceptance follows common knowledge about how to define and secure legal rights. This position is ideological: it is a political stance that they use to position themselves. They thus have an a priori understanding of justice with regard to economics.

Agarwal and Folbre reinvestigate how women's legal rights, or what they think should be women's legal rights, are violated in practice. They investigate what causes the lack of equal rights in law, custom, and culture. The gender gap, dichotomy of gender roles, hierarchical power over and against women, class, and caste are the factors most frequently cited by the authors to explain inequality between men and women.[53]

For Agarwal, the lack of implementation of legal rights for land is the most obvious and important cause of women's lack of economic autonomy. Agarwal advocates that rights to claim land be upheld by the rule of law in the community where they would be realized.[54] Political authorities have ways and means to establish the same rights for women and men. A just political system will put women's and men's rights on the agenda and make sure that rights are distributed in a just manner regardless of gender, as is the intention in the 1950 Indian Constitution. If this doesn't happen, the result is gender inequity and an unjust or inefficient political system. A fair and egalitarian legal and political framework is fundamental for a functioning democracy—and democracy is fundamental to alleviating some of the burdens of the poor.[55] Awareness of all the well-intended agreements that already exist to secure equal rights for women could amount to a tremendous consciousness-raising.[56]

Seventh, there is *justice*. The work of these feminist economists points squarely at causes for women's oppression in economics. They in turn are caused by the social construction of gender, class issues, race issues, lack of rights, lack of equality, biased economic science, and cultural marginalization of women. Although they come from various social, religious, and cultural sources, their result seems to be the same: the economic disempowerment of women. The feminist economists universally evince a consistent concern that certain values undergird women's economic situation, and this is a sign of aspirations toward justice. Several of the feminist economists also use justice and theories of justice in their discourse.

In spite of differences in approach and scholarly work, the commonality among the authors and texts analyzed are more important than their differences. They all consider economics as a social construction and are critical of its gender blindness, mathematical dogmatism, lack of a true empirical basis, and ignorance of real problems.

Can a feminist liberation theology, one that is formed in the field of feminist ethics, clarify the claims for justice made by feminist economists? To find out, our focus turns now to feminist ethicists and their treatment of economic justice in the context of feminist liberation theology and feminist theory.

PART TWO

FEMINIST ETHICS

4

LIBERATION THEOLOGY
AND FEMINISM

My focus now shifts from feminist economists to Christian feminist ethicists and their perspectives on economic justice. This chapter analyzes how theologians and feminist ethicists have wrestled with liberation theology in general and economic justice in particular. The chapters that follow explore how feminist ethics can deepen and clarify ethical concepts used by feminist economists.

Christian theology is not exactly spoiled by success stories. Liberation theology and feminist theology are rare exceptions in that they have attained recognition and approval in many circles outside of the theological family.[1] With the emergence of the terms *liberation* and *feminist*, theology stopped being spelled with a capital *T*. Theology was no longer seen as a single, unified subject that would deliver definite answers to ultimate questions but as a particular handicraft for particular situations or contexts. This development is in and of itself a major contribution to the theological enterprise.

Several feminist theologians have been informed and inspired by liberation theology and position themselves in relation to liberation theology.[2] Liberation theology is known for its demand for radical social change in order to improve the conditions of the oppressed. What is it about liberation theology that provides inspiration and information for feminist theology and, in particular, feminist theological ethics?

Liberation theology and feminist theology grew in the same time period and have common sources of inspiration. They also share an opposition to oppressive economic, social, cultural, and political structures. While theology used to have its starting point exclusively in Scripture, tradition, and philosophical reasoning, liberation theology leans on a different method, in which praxis and experience are given central positions on a par with Scripture.[3] There has been a tremendous growth of theologies that have taken a particular context as a starting point for reflection; feminist theology is but one of those. Also, within feminist theology there are now many variations, such as womanist theology, *mujerista* theology, Asian women's theology, and African women's theology.[4]

For example, when Katie G. Cannon is invited to speak on the topic "The Womanist Dilemma in the Development of a Black Liberation Ethics," she is concerned about how black women are omitted from black liberation theology. She argues that, since male black theologians readily accept what is presented to them in their theological training and lack a critical consciousness that includes women, black women are made invisible in their work.[5]

Pedagogy of the Oppressed

Paulo Freire, a Brazilian educator and a founder of the liberationist approach to literacy, stands out for both his pedagogical and theoretical analysis of oppression, and also for his classic work, *Pedagogy of the Oppressed*.[6] His main idea was to involve people at the grassroots level and educate them so that they would develop a sense of critical consciousness. Each person in the community must develop critical consciousness, he argued, and it will provide each individual with the necessary means to analyze an oppressive situation and suggest means to overcome oppression. The notion that every individual could and should develop a critical consciousness is important for understanding the attraction of Freire's pedagogy to the political left.

If people understand how oppressive structures dehumanize them, they are in a better position to transform these structures, recognize ignorance, and increase humanization for both themselves and their oppressors. In some cases they manage to take on a leadership role. The basic contradiction for Freire is between the humanizing and the dehumanizing forces that affect people. Both the oppressed and the oppressors are caught in dehumanizing structures of injustice, alienation, lack of freedom, and ignorance. But this is not destiny. It can be changed if a critical consciousness is developed.[7] The oppressed must realize that they should not identify with the dehumanizing practice of the oppressors but change practices that are oppressive. Identification with the oppressors is tempting and dangerous: learning to be critical is liberating and difficult.[8] To accomplish liberation, one must be on the side of humanization, opposing all that is dehumanizing.[9]

Gustavo Gutiérrez, a Peruvian Catholic priest and theologian, was a contemporary of Freire and is best known for his work *A Theology of Liberation*.[10] Gutiérrez made connections between the impact of the political upheaval in the 1970s in Latin America and Marxist theory.[11]

Gutiérrez argued that the need for improvement for oppressed people is urgent and there are no other options for the poor than to try to organize a social revolution. The version of liberation that Gutiérrez advocated was firmly rooted in the Bible and a materialist analysis of the modes of production as well as in a thorough understanding of the alienation that was brought about by structures that estrange the worker. The landless and the people without power and ownership of the means of production must seek venues to better their circumstances. Gutiérrez wrote:

> Only a radical break from the status quo, that is, a profound transformation of the private property system, access to power of the exploited class, and a social revolution that would break this dependency would allow for the change to a new society, a socialist society—or at least allow that such a society might be possible.[12]

Utilizing "base communities" is a means to encourage and improve the critical consciousness of the poor while introducing them to a reading of the Bible that increases their self-esteem as well as their options for a better future. This form of Bible reading is closely connected to a Marxist understanding of political change and economic development.

Gutiérrez denounced the mainstream concept of development, which he thought had been too heavily influenced by the dominating powers; he preferred to talk about liberation because the traditional definition of development revolved around goods that the beneficial rich countries bestow on the poor. Gutiérrez denounced a patriarchal attitude toward the oppressed by the oppressors. However, he failed to see the connection between this attitude and how women are subjugated in Latin American cultures.

Not only economic factors but also cultural, social, and political aspects of life must be included in the concept of liberation, suggested Gutiérrez. Ultimately, he strove for an "emancipation of man in history."[13] The agency of individual persons is key to radical change and his stress on the individual is important to note, since liberation theology's view of the human person is more complex than Marxist theory allows. Gutiérrez utilized psychoanalysis as well as philosophy to develop a view of humans in a process of "permanent cultural revolution."[14] The Christian understanding of human nature has many interpretations, but to say that human beings are only a product of their material surroundings and the mode of production is not enough for Gutiérrez. Free will is inherent in Christian understanding of human persons, as is the human capacity to love and to do justice.

Radical Social Change

In its early days, liberation theology in itself was a significant change in theology, and it allied religious thought to social change. It provided an example of a creative and radical approach to justice and social change. At the time, the prevalent theological and dogmatic discourse in Latin America was on the brink of implosion by internal lack of movement and unquestioning obedience to the authorities.

John C. Bennett was one of North America's great Christian realists and, as such, was cautious about what liberation theology could offer in the long run since its vision outstripped its grasp of the complexities of human nature.[15] Yet, Bennett was a champion of liberation theology. In *The Radical Imperative,* Bennett described the church in Latin America as hopelessly stale and totally accommodated to Latin American society. Therefore, liberation theology as presented by Gutiérrez represented for Bennett a profound and radical renewal of theology and an inspiration to theology in both its Protestant and Catholic strands.[16]

Important similarities exist between feminist liberation theology and Latin American liberation theology in their push for radical social change. It is mainly this aim that draws feminist theologians to Latin American liberation theology. A revolutionary spirit was heralded by Latin American liberation theologians, some of whom were prepared to support even armed revolt.[17] Immediate change, at any cost, was in some quarters not too high a price in face of the severe and even deadly oppression they experienced.[18] In his foreword to *Pedagogy of the Oppressed,* theologian Richard Shaull commends the book for its focus on the lethargic condition of the poor, a condition that Freire showed a way to change.

Freire provided a method for the oppressed to struggle for justice. People are to be approached as subjects who can change the world. Shaull notes that the technologically advanced Western world is quickly making objects of people. Therefore, he recommends Freire's pedagogy also to intellectuals in the West. Shaull himself exhibits his revolutionary leanings in both theology and politics.[19]

There is a growing consensus among feminist liberation theologians that women's liberation from oppressive patriarchy is a goal. Further, all feminist liberation theologians express themselves as being in solidarity with oppressed people, regardless of biological sex, ethnicity, sexual preference, class, age, handicap, or other characteristics that occasion their oppression or diminish their options. For liberation to take place, social change that brings about justice is necessary. But here the consensus ends.

Feminist theologies harbor many different opinions about the shape of liberation and how it ought to take place. I limit my inquiry to how economic oppression affects women. The main differences between feminist liberation theologians run along the ideological lines of liberal feminism, radical feminism, and socialist feminism.[20] Liberal feminists are fundamentally concerned about equal social and political rights for women. Radical feminists tend to stress the problems inherent in a patriarchal world order. Socialist feminists tend to look at how oppressive economic and social orders discriminate against women.[21] As for methods, norms, and concepts to obtain liberation, there is no consensus.

Social Change in Theory and Method

Two foundational points of liberation methodology stand out: praxis and Scripture. The crucial objective, to achieve social change and improve justice, dictates changes in traditional theological method. It brings to the fore increased concern for those who suffer oppression.

In order for these changes to occur, method must be inclusive and give weight to the insights presented by the people concerned. The preferential position of the oppressed is a given and their stories are taken seriously. Called the "preferential option for the poor," this position means, among other things, that the living conditions of the poor are so oppressive and exploitative as to demand priority for change.[22]

Argentinian theologian José Míguez Bonino is forthright in his theological claims to distributive justice. He writes: "The basic ethical criterion, or principle of justice, is 'the maximizing of universal human possibilities and the minimizing of human costs.'"[23] A utilitarian element is there in his theory, but he also adheres to an overriding norm. The preferential option for the poor is the norm he uses to estimate what should be distributed and to whom. For him, it is not enough to achieve happiness for the many; the poor should have priority. He supports his ethics by asserting that a claim for justice is inherent in Christian theology—a position known as the "eschatological position" of liberation theology.[24]

In liberation theology, praxis is closely connected to the experience of oppression and also to how oppression is reflected in Scripture. This is not an original Marxist understanding of praxis. In Marxist theory, little attention is placed on the individual; emphasis is on the collective group. Praxis is related to work: through work you learn about your situation in life and how it is related to Marxist theory, that is, whether you are an alienated person or not. Liberation theology has expanded the concept of praxis to include experiences of personal faith. Since the individual has a central position in all Christian theology, it is hard to avoid a clear split between Christian and Marxist theory regarding the individual and spiritual life. Yet the combination of praxis and experience, with its inclusion of personal stories, has proved powerful and provides for a close relationship between feminist theology and liberation theology. Both theologies aim for liberation from forms of oppression. Who denies or delivers this liberation? Is liberation a right that women and the poor have? If freedom and certain benefits are rights that people have, it is usually assumed that some institution must exist that will uphold the rights. The *prima facie* status for liberation, especially if defined as freedom, seems strong since there are few who think it necessary to argue for why the oppressed have the right to be liberated.

Still, for a claimed right to be meaningful and valid, there must be someone or something that is able to deliver the goods. How can one claim one's right to a good if no institution or court can uphold the claim?[25] Even religiously based claims require some such framework. If God is the benefactor, for example, it is well known that God is slow when it comes to delivering goods. Religious claims, grounded in Scripture or the kingdom of God, may inform behavior and may sustain hope in the abstract. This hope can activate creativity and compassion so that people speak out about the lack of rights and demand rights for the poor. Still, the delivery does not come from the godhead in any way that anyone can prove empirically. Rights to goods must be proximately claimed somewhere else. Welfare states tend to be concerned about the distribution of basic economic goods to their citizens. The justification for rights in welfare states has an ideological source. In sustainable political systems, claimed rights depend on the opinion of a majority of the voters; all citizens should have basic needs met whether they manage this on their own or not. Rights are never self-evident; and they must always be claimed, argued for, and upheld. In the end, rights to goods require the means to be provided for. If the state, the community, or the personal network fails to provide for the basic needs that are apprehended as rights, there are hardly any courts of appeal. The welfare state is a fragile construction whose stability demands democratic and civil support and sufficient provision through taxes on labor, wealth, goods, and enterprises. If there is no institution, no political system, and no religious system that delivers freedom and meets the claim rights of the oppressed, the task is to create this mechanism.

Hermeneutics in Liberation Theology

Hermeneutics, or the theory of interpretation, plays an important role in liberation theology's analysis of social and spiritual life. Without interpretation, how can one understand what is happening and, even more important, what needs to be changed? The "hermeneutics of suspicion" developed by theologian Juan Luis Segundo has been widely accepted as a means to uncover covert repressive situations and ideologies.

An independent point of view from which one can analyze the world through hermeneutics is what Segundo was looking for.[26] He put forth faith as a position that does not adhere to any particular position and has its foundation in ultimate values and ideas. He assumed that a faith position can therefore be used to evaluate ideologies that are themselves blind to their own weaknesses, while they may be very accurate in their critique of other ideologies. Since faith has no particular stance in secular ideologies and systems, he advocated that faith engender a critical interpretation and analysis.[27]

Segundo's hermeneutics of suspicion starts from an ideology of suspicion.[28] First, ideology should always include an element of suspicion toward church and society. Second, a hermeneutics of suspicion should include a phenomenological analysis of structures and theology. Third, a "hermeneutical circle" (that is, the living dialogue of text and interpretation) can incorporate suspicion into the most common and important interpretation of the Bible. Out of those considerations grows a new hermeneutics with new principles for interpreting the Bible. From this understanding, new ideologies and praxis grow.[29]

American theologian Thomas Schubeck takes Segundo's faith stance seriously. A faith stance imparts a critical distance from both secular and theological ideologies. This faith stance is open also to the theological enterprise to maintain its critical distance. It is easy to understand the need for and usefulness of a position that stands on its own foundation. Yet, to claim that adherence to ultimate values and norms will provide an independent position, disconnected from secular and theological ideologies, seems to be a far-reaching assumption. Faith and adherence to ultimate values and norms may, in good times, give some space to a new perspective, but not enough to change the whole understanding involved in the hermeneutics of suspicion. It may be more effective to make one's ideological stance clear and then compare it with one's hermeneutics of suspicion. As this ideological position is bound to change as well, the system is not so clear-cut as it might first appear to be.

Gutiérrez gives a concrete biblical example of a hermeneutics of suspicion that favors the poor. He cites the figure of Job as an example of a person who, with the utmost integrity, refuses to admit that what happens to him is related to sins that he has committed. Although he does not claim to be without sin, Job will admit no direct correlation between the misery that he is put through and what his behavior deserves. Gutiérrez makes many valid points about Job's steadfast position: Job speaks about God in new ways and demands that God speak to him. Job sees his sins in perspective. He favors good treatment of the poor. And he will not abandon his integrity or give in to his friends and their traditional thinking that Job must have done something to cause his misery.[30] That individuals have the freedom and the obligation to interpret their own situation and talk to God about it is an implicit assumption in Gutiérrez's interpretation. Personal experience is taken seriously in understanding where one is situated in relationship to God. We are faced with a story of great intensity and beauty in which the main character is suspicious of the interpretation of his experience offered by wise men and friends. He doubts that the circumstances that brought him down are just: he is suspicious about the God who puts him in the situation, and he finds new ways to talk about God that are directly related to his own experience.

Feminist theologian Elisabeth Schüssler Fiorenza represents a feminist critical hermeneutics.[31] In one aspect of her work, she makes use of Elizabeth Cady Stanton's *The Woman's Bible* (1895, 1898) to develop her thesis.[32] Fiorenza recalls Stanton's point about the massive impact that the Bible had on the lives of women and yet how women were totally absent from the work of exegesis. (Stanton's own focus was not on theology, but on society.) If the lives of women depended to such an extent on what was preached from the pulpit and thought in the churches, she argued, women had an obligation to reflect on it.[33] The whole interpretive perspective of women was absent in Scripture, in tradition, in theology, and in church history. While post-Christian theologian-philosopher Mary Daly has chosen a route to exile herself from the theological paradigm altogether, Fiorenza argues that the perspective of women has such validity that it must be included in the theological paradigm in order to change it and transform Christian theological thinking. In her view, the Bible isn't an archetype for thinking about theology, but rather a prototype of something that happens continuously.[34] One important tool to accomplish this inclusion is to develop a hermeneutics so that women cannot be excluded anymore. Fiorenza has developed her own position, in part, into a feminist hermeneutics of suspicion.

Unlike Gutiérrez, Fiorenza is not satisfied with new ways of looking at the text. She wants to analyze not only the text itself but also the social conditions at the time, the relationship between women and men, and women's place in society and in the contemporary world.[35] Her work offers numerous examples of such interpretation and the radical transformation it entails in individuals, the church, the academy, and society.

Focus on the Oppressed

The arena of oppression is vast indeed. Oppression comes in different forms and shapes. There exists a continuum of forms and intensity of oppression, and it is necessary to be aware of this when looking at how liberation theologians and feminist ethicists address oppression. Oppression can be all-encompassing, as in slavery, but oppression as a concept is difficult to measure.

When analyzing oppression, one might think that the analysis aims at something that is well known. If the person herself is defining oppression, she might be able to give her version of what it entails. And that is one perspective. But who are those that can rightfully identify themselves as oppressed? What about the person who is not allowed to jump across buildings for pleasure or money and who may consider this a form of oppression against personal freedom to do whatever does not harm anyone else?

One important practice in the women's liberation movement has been to let the people concerned define their own situation. This inductive and time-consuming way of learning is key. Liberation theologians include economic, political, and cultural oppression in their analysis of oppression, but they also include religious and spiritual oppression. Every group—women, blacks, lesbians, the unemployed, children, and the elderly—has the right to tell its story and not to be questioned on what it considers to be true.

At the center of oppression is power or the lack thereof. Hannah Arendt defined power as having the potential to act or speak in a certain way.[36] But power is not a condition or a state, like strength. If one loses one's potential for power, as she called it, then someone else gains the power to decide what is necessary for one's survival. Feminist liberation ethics must find ways to argue for an ethical approach that makes women's lack of "power potential" obvious.

To put ethics before profit in the global household is a crucial demand for the liberation of women. So, when theorizing about oppression, it is not enough to stay at the personal level. Oppression most often connotes something greater that is missing yet could give people a sense of dignity and freedom. In Arendt's terms, it is a lack of potential for power.

Oppression is not having the power to make decisions because constraints force us to do things that we would not have chosen. Constraints exacerbate the lack of power and, as Nancy Folbre discusses, constraints can originate with gender, class, sexual preference, age, and nationality (see chapter 3). Political constraints on women's own bodies are a well-documented field.[37] Lack of control of the means to support oneself is something that many women experience as disempowering. The powerlessness of not knowing where one's daily bread will come from, or if it will come, is less than dignifying.

If this powerlessness is what defines oppression, then what is liberation? Liberation on a personal level is connected to individual agency—the space in which the individual has control and can make decisions. In that space, liberties and freedoms can be exercised. As with all else, there are only degrees of liberation. The condition of liberation is never achieved in a full and sustained manner. New forms of oppression surface regularly and demand a response: liberation is a never-ending process.

No Gender Analysis

As late as 1993, Schubeck analyzed the impact on ethics made by liberation theology. Schubeck acknowledges very little information about gender in liberation theology. Even this late, he only names the most well known feminist theologians, such as Fiorenza, Rosemary Radford Ruether, and Beverly W. Harrison, as women who have related themselves to this strand of theology and also improved it. But his acknowledgment ends there.[38] The list of feminist theologians who would recognize influences from Latin American liberation theology is much longer.

Despite such influence, feminist critiques of liberation theology have been fierce. Mary E. Hunt argued that liberation theology was oblivious to issues of sex.[39] The first theologians writing liberation theology were men, and most of those were educated in Europe before returning to Latin America. Class, rather than gender, was the category for their analysis of society. Feminists have argued that class, while a valid category, is insufficient.

The place of women in early liberation theology was not particularly different than it was in any other form of theology at the time. The double oppression of women was not a subject in early liberation theology, and there is nothing to show that this was even reflected upon until women theologians from Latin America started their own theologizing. Liberation theology by women is an active area at the present time.

Eclectic Feminism

Feminist liberation theology has many influences. To obtain radical change, all kinds of insights from theology, social sciences, human sciences, and natural sciences can and do contribute. To reformulate the human dilemma of living in a world burdened with many conflicts and shortcomings, much needs to be known and known in new ways to overcome the oppressive powers that affect the lives of people—women as well as men.

Women of color, working-class women, women of all religions, all cultures, women who love women, and women who love men must all be included in the process of radical change. Insights from many disciplines are needed; for example, insights from child psychology—from Melanie Klein and the object-relations theory to Jean Piaget and his ideas about how children mature—have been used to determine how the feminine and masculine genders are formed and constructed.

Conceptions of women's moral development have played a major role in understanding and evaluating how women make decisions in ethical matters. Out of this analysis developed the difference and sameness debate that includes the question of whether or not women and men are essentially different in nature.[40] To put it mildly, this is not a new question to theology, yet the recognition in theology of women as full human persons is still not achieved. To take but one instance of how women remain somehow less than men in religious circles, the latest consideration of women's ordination was dismissed by the Roman Catholic Church on the grounds that women are unable to represent Christ in full.

A great many advances have been made by feminist-inspired scholars, scientists, and theologians: knowledge about violence against women has grown, as has knowledge about relationships in the human community between women and women, men and women, women and children, men and children, those with power, and those without power. Yet, the situation of the have-nots in relationship to the haves is better known, but there is still no common opinion of what to do about it.

The Ethical Imperative

Feminist theology and liberation theology share a common perspective of the oppressed and an aim to end oppression. They utilize the experiences of the oppressed and are informed by Marxist critical theory in their political analysis.

At the center of a culture of the oppressed is the massive experience and knowledge that the oppressed have of oppression and about the oppressor. It is a matter of survival to know what happens at this center. For the oppressed to survive and improve their condition, it will always be crucial to know the rules, values, and culture that are transmitted by those in power.

Liberation theology's answer to oppression is liberation, which is achieved through the difficult process of humanization for both oppressor and oppressed:

> Liberation is thus a childbirth, and a painful one. The *man* who emerges is a new *man*, viable only as the oppressor-oppressed contradiction is superseded by the humanization of all *men*. Or to put it another way, the solution of this contradiction is born in the labor which brings into the

world this new *man:* no longer oppressor nor longer oppressed, but *man* in the process of achieving freedom.[41] (Italics mine)

To recognize and support the "preferential option for the poor," which liberation theology calls for, is the result of a choice of perspective, not a claim to ultimate truth or an effort to settle an epistemological question. But those whose lives have been governed by the rich and powerful have an experience that scientists, politicians, and activists must ask about and be informed by. Even if it turns out that their experience is like the experience of people in power, it is something that must be explored and not assumed. If it turns out that experiences between women and men, poor and rich, and those in the center and those in the periphery are different, those differences need to be analyzed.

Advancing a political position that gives priority to freedom and personal agency for the oppressed is a position that has been developed in feminist theory. In addition to the oppression exercised by patriarchy, feminist theory considers economic deprivation and cultural, social, and political oppression.[42] In this work, insufficiency of analytical tools became an issue of major importance. How could one rely on the social analysis or understand the context of oppression or learn from experiences, if the unequal distribution of power between genders was not considered? Even liberation theology neglected women's experience and perspectives. The exclusive use of masculine pronouns in liberation theology exemplified the discipline's neglect of the oppression of women. Yet it still holds a strong attraction for those who want to understand the imperatives and mechanisms of social change and improvement in the lives of the oppressed.

Liberation theology is well known outside the theological enterprise, as is feminist theology. Yet, in spite of the fact that many of the issues involved in these theologies are *ethical* problems, they have not brought forth a tremendous amount of work in ethics as *ethics,* even though they have abounded in arguments for ethical reevaluation. At the heart of feminist and liberation theology, a claim for liberation from oppression and attainment of justice, are ethical imperatives.

Both justice and liberation are objectives given through the will of God to be achieved in history. In the next two chapters, I present the specifically ethical work of feminist liberation theology to find out what feminists ethics can contribute to the task of improving economic justice.

5

FEMINIST ETHICS AND ECONOMICS

How can ethicists pose moral questions of a science that does not overtly occupy itself with ethical issues? Can the discipline of ethics legitimately argue that economics, as a scientific occupation and as a practice, has any obligation to solve problems such as poverty? Common sense might assume that it does, but my concern here is to develop the theoretical and ethical grounds on which we can proceed.

One way to proceed is to explore the dialectic between justice and economics. For this purpose, I engage the work of Beverly Wildung Harrison, a pioneer in Christian feminist ethics. I outline her contribution to economic justice and her analysis of economic theory, and I use her work to develop ethical arguments in feminist economics.

At that juncture, feminist theory and critical theory come into play to strengthen and make more plausible the theoretical and ethical underpinnings of feminist economics. Can an ethics derived from feminist liberation theology establish principles that enable neoclassical economic theory to dialogue with justice discourse? Assuming that the ethical discourse of feminist liberation theology is about radical social change, as pointed out in the last chapter, which arguments can support change in economic theory and practice so that exploitative and oppressive structures can be critically analyzed and changed?

Hard ethical questions must be asked of the economic sciences in response to massive poverty on earth.

Feminist Ethics: Founding Ideas

As a feminist socialist, Harrison expresses her conviction that a historical, dialectical method, devoted to socialism and economic democracy, will have much to contribute to our political and economic problems.[1] Her ethical insights bring many new perspectives to feminist liberation theology and are indeed a valuable source to enhance our arguments in ethics about economics.

Harrison has developed her own perspective in dialogue with the work of theologians Reinhold Niebuhr and John C. Bennett. Bennett urged new generations to concentrate on the field of economics and social theory. He argued that we must "urge a new generation of persons concerned about Christian ethics to press the socialistic questions even though they do not accept ready-made socialistic answers. A new debate is needed about economic institutions and on a much more fundamental level."[2]

Harrison is also critical about their contributions and thus utilizes new sources for her ethical reflection—mostly material from social sciences and liberation and feminist theology.

Among the feminist theologians who have influenced her work are Dorothee Soelle, Carter Heyward, Nelle Morton, and Rosemary Radford Ruether. She is also well versed in Latin American liberation theology and the tradition of feminist liberation theologians. Within the discipline of feminist theology, she is one of the few with a keen sense of political issues. She assumes that the social order can change and justice can be attained, and that ensuring this must become a preoccupation for feminist liberation theologians and ethicists.

Liberal Theology and Empiricism

Liberal theology arose among theologians who wanted major social changes in the late nineteenth and early twentieth centuries. They thought it possible to bring about the reign of God here and now by living a good, Christlike life.[3] But, for reasons well researched by Ernst Troeltsch, such change did not come about.[4]

The United States version of liberal theology, which engendered the Social Gospel Movement, emphasized people's experience and sought real political change. Harrison builds in part on this liberal theological legacy. She maintains that it did contribute significantly to ethical and theological discourse. It allowed for inclusion of worldly matters in theological arguments. It was an intellectually candid theology concerned with scientific knowledge. It recognized that theological understanding changes within history and that people have the freedom and power to change the course of events.[5] All of these assumptions also underpin feminist theology and feminist theory.

Harrison on Niebuhr

As a student of Reinhold Niebuhr, the most influential Christian ethicist in the United States during the last century, Harrison makes it her task to review and critique some of his teaching about social justice.

To correct what was taught by liberal theology and the Social Gospel Movement, Niebuhr argued for an ethical perspective which has become known as "Christian realism." Human community, according to Niebuhr, will not be able to create the reign of God within the parameters of history, since we are part of a fallen and sinful world. People behave in ways that are incongruent with the common good as well as their own personal good. In social psychology, this is considered dysfunctional behavior, or "cognitive dissonance."[6] In addition, Niebuhr noted, even those who confess Christian faith do not manage to live according to the teachings of Jesus.[7] In the Letter of Paul to the Romans, Paul considers this to be sin—pure and simple. According to Niebuhr, there are few signs that human nature will improve, or that we will be able to create what we most want.[8] Against this backdrop stands the reality of grace and the central Christian ideal of loving self-sacrifice.

Ethicist Karen Lebacqz has also looked at the earlier work of Niebuhr and found that his main contribution to Christian ethics is that he asks questions about justice, the reasons for justice, and the failure to achieve justice. The outcome of sin is injustice and, since sin is unlikely to go away, justice is at a disadvantage.[9] But Niebuhr does not succeed in his efforts to define justice. This could, in fact, be advantageous, since the rules that he does provide open up the results of his work for continuous reassessment. He struggles on with the justice concept, finding no final solution.[10]

For Niebuhr, the first criterion for justice is a balance of power. The centers of powers must be recognized: economic power is one center and political power is the other, and they will balance each other. On this score, Harrison is particularly critical. She finds it detrimental to Christian ethics that such an ahistorical analysis of power has had such major influence on the development of ethical work on economics in the United States.[11]

Two ethical values stand out in Niebuhr's work: freedom and equality. Freedom is innate to human nature and there can be no justice without freedom. Equality is the value that is a corrective to freedom in respect to justice. If freedom violates equality, freedom must be adjusted to increase equality. In this sense, equality supersedes freedom as the more important value.[12]

One failure of political realism is that it lacks a full understanding of the role economics plays in society. Even though there were indications in

Niebuhr's earlier work of the importance of economics, he never fulfilled his analysis; and he drops the issue in his later writing. Niebuhr was convinced that politics would control the economy and influence economic policy through the democratic process.[13] Later in his life, his focus changed from economic to political power.[14] In addition to his blindness to the shortcomings of political realism, Niebuhr had an ongoing polemic against Marxist social theory. While at one point intrigued and inspired by the concepts in Marxist theory, Niebuhr underwent a major change in his assessment of Marxism and became an astute critic. He turned against Marxist theory and its potential use within Christian social ethics.[15]

Harrison first encountered Marxism as a student of Niebuhr at the time when he had turned away from Marxism. She is convinced that he knew very little of Marx's writing firsthand.[16] Niebuhr did misrepresent Marx when he read him as an idealist like himself, and he wrongly assumed Marx was a scientific positivist. Simplistic critique against Marx on charges of scientific determinism is something that Harrison rejects. Instead, she places Marx in the context of the nineteenth-century discussion of the task of social sciences. For Marx, praxis, actual conflicts, and tensions were to be put into historic context. He was convinced that economics could be changed through collective action. Studying what was going on with a critical eye and an open mind was a goal for Marx, and for this reason, he was the founder of critical theory. In his thinking about economics, Marx stressed labor rather than capital. He was extremely critical toward existing theories of political economy as something ruled by natural law. He refused to see buying and selling as the basis for economic activity, and he was critical of the pretensions of scientific political economy in his time.[17] The function of the reigning schools of scientific political economy, Marx argued, was covertly to legitimize capitalism with its consequent detrimental effects on society and labor.

According to Harrison, Niebuhr was also misinformed when he assumed that Marx wanted to construct a philosophy of history. Marx was opposed to such theories and instead wanted to study history from a practical point of view. For Niebuhr, Marx's project was bad religion, and this provided him with a convenient excuse not to study the Marxist critique of religion or to take Marx seriously as a social theoretician.[18]

Harrison analyzes the use of the concept *realism*. In many quarters, the excuse for not addressing major radical change is that such change is not "realistic." So the complex social system does not get sufficiently analyzed. The idea of realism takes precedence over radical social theory and its potential for change. Ironically, what actually goes on—what is "real"— does not enter into the discussion of realism.[19]

Niebuhr's alliance with political theory rather than social sciences is rarely questioned. His concept of political realism has not been sufficiently analyzed. Niebuhr adheres to a notion about power as an independent force available to those individuals and groups who are interested.[20] According to Harrison, this is an idealistic and ahistorical analysis of how power functions in society. To Harrison, the strength of radical social theory lies in its focus on actual social problems, not on ideas. The task of "moral reasoning is neither causual/predictive nor critical/descriptive, but evaluative/transformative; it aims to assess how our actions may affect a situation for the better."[21]

As noted above, Niebuhr was convinced that a democratic political process would be able to control the economy.[22] In the prevailing liberal academic tradition, large parts of Christian ethics and social sciences have accepted a market economy with global aspirations. Niebuhr did understand power in a very limited fashion, restricted to the political scene. He opposed Marx's theory that a capitalist mode of production shapes society and results in antagonistic social relations between classes.[23]

Niebuhr's underestimation of economic realities leaves economic theory outside his analysis of the social paradigm. To Harrison this is one explanation why, in the midst of economic growth and internationalization, Christian ethics has remained relatively tranquil and accommodating. Christian ethicists lack the necessary tools to analyze urgent problems in political economics. Meanwhile, the political debate is filled with hardcore neoclassical economic and scientific assumptions. The only serious challenge to neoclassical theory is neo-Marxist political economics, which many Christian ethicists have already ruled out.[24]

Neoclassical economics has established its goal as utility and profit maximization. Moral questions, such as just distribution, are factors extrinsic to the theory. Traditional Christian ethics is complicit, Harrison believes. Accepting such a limited paradigm for social analysis is a major obstacle to any radical change. The gap between liberal economic theory and praxis is growing.[25]

Niebuhr recommends that ethicists do their best to reason about the common good. To create the perfect and just living conditions portrayed by Christian love is not realistic, but ethicists can still keep the quest for justice at the center of ethical discourse. Compromises will always be necessary while looking for the best possible solutions. Compromises are inevitable even if they compromise consciences. To obtain the next best thing, when better alternatives are beyond reach, compromises are necessary.

Harrison, a student but also critic of Niebuhr, disagrees with Niebuhr's negative anthropology and negative understanding of human nature. Niebuhr questions human capacity to create a just society.[26] Also, for Niebuhr, love is the moving force in the work of justice as well as the ultimate ideal in Christian ethics. Love provides a perspective or a position from the outside from which justice can be evaluated.[27] But, as people, we will never be able to exercise the ideal of love in a consistent manner. There exists a dialectical relationship between love and justice in Niebuhr's thinking. Since love cannot be realized and justice can never be perfect, there is a dialogue between them that can improve understanding of justice.[28] In this process, Niebuhr is willing to give what we today call an "epistemological privilege to the poor." He writes, "Those who benefit from social injustice are naturally less capable of understanding its real character than those who suffer from it."[29]

The "love and right relations" perspective that Harrison advocates in this dispute seems more plausible than Niebuhr's.[30] To respect people as mature moral beings and expect that moral conduct will be good and will improve indicates that there is something in every person that makes it possible to improve. The oppressive powers that stand against goodness and righteousness have deprived so many of so much for so long that it is imperative to recognize and encourage demands for justice. It is not fair to say that because of human fallibility it cannot be done.

Learning from Social Sciences

Harrison strongly advocates that ethicists acquire good knowledge of the social sciences and policy issues in ethical discourse. Relevant ethical dialogue is based on knowledge of issues and in the reality and lives of actual people. To listen to what is said by the people who are affected by ideology, culture, prejudices, exploitation, and degradation—that is, to listen to the oppressed—is a necessity if justice is to be attained. Harrison presents the problem as one of method. To be able to integrate an appropriate ethics, we must turn to social sciences for adequate information regarding what causes hardship, exploitation, oppression, and other forms of injustice. This requires hard interdisciplinary work. Christian theologians often avoid such interdisciplinary work, preferring to call on authorities like Niebuhr for guidelines.[31]

And so Christian ethics is barren in the field of economics and radical social change. Often, the discussion gets stuck right here. Harrison suggests that, to move forward, we must focus on the ideological issues at hand. Theologians must be "self-conscious about how ideology shapes the social scientific and philosophical theory we incorporate into ethical reflection."[32] Those who undertake ethical analysis and are unaware of or not outspoken about their ideological position will undermine and thwart their own ambitions to be objective.

Social sciences such as economics convert our norms and form our understanding of social policy and ideology without much analysis coming forth from ethicists. Critical social theory is virtually ignored, and the void of critical analysis undermines our ability to change what we do not like. The fine line between what is possible and what is not is extremely difficult to draw because there is no way to have all the relevant information. It is particularly difficult to predict what will happen tomorrow. A quick glance at the stock market makes this amazingly clear.

What Harrison hopes for is increased knowledge and improved analyses so that ethicists and theologians can make better predictions. The difference between Harrison and Niebuhr centers on this crucial issue: Will humankind be able to progress more than at present? Should a positive perspective take precedence over a negative perspective regarding human nature? Here they draw different conclusions: Harrison is optimistic, Niebuhr is "realistic."

Critical theory developed in feminist theory has expanded the historical-materialist understanding of how people are positioned in society and the kind of effects this has on the construction of human nature. A feminist-socialist view of human nature includes material circumstances—for example, one's class position, what kind of work one has, whether a person shares resources, and historical circumstances such as culture, experiences, gender, and age. All these factors contribute to the construction of human nature.[33] They also play into how gender is constructed.

I understand the undercurrent in feminist theory, in all its diversity, to move toward the possibility of improvement of the human project. The possible change and improvement of the construction of human nature are one major factor in the positive expectation in social change. Being a historical materialist within feminism, Harrison makes a connection between the concrete human situation and the social construction of human nature. And she allows herself to be optimistic on this score. Her optimism is founded in social science, her personal ideology, and advanced welfare states that have proven themselves viable.

My analytical task in respect to economic ethics requires a comment on the question of ideology. While Harrison makes a clear argument for the inclusion of ideology in ethical analysis, it seems that this inclusion is geared toward the implementation of normative ethics, not to its theoretical stage. While Harrison and others are certain that there can be no ethics in "economics proper," they do not show why this is the case.

If it is assumed for ideological reasons that it is impossible to change the economic system, it is a waste of time to analyze economics in ethical terms. It seems more advantageous, then, to analyze economics—its own internal logic—apart from ideology. If the analysis is conducted with distinct ideological presuppositions, the result is already made up. To transform an economic system so that it can be more inclusive of the poor, an open-minded search for ethical guidance is required, with the understanding that there are ideological conditions for how the result will be implemented and interpreted once it is achieved.

Critical Theory and Radical Social Theory

Critical theory has been an important part of the development of feminist theory,[34] and feminist philosophers have taken up the issues.[35]

Harrison understands social theory as a general knowledge of social theories of all kinds, a good acquaintance with how society actually works in all its complexity, and versatility in economics, political science, sociology, and psychology. All the most common liberal connotations seem to rely on this concept: we assume that we live in an open, equal, and just society, and with the help of social theory we can rectify any unfortunate mistakes and can solve all problems.

To find out what distinguishes critical social theory from radical theory is not easy when looking at Harrison's text. Presumably, they are really not different to her. At the heart of radicalism is the willingness to change in a radical manner what is wrong or unjust. When Harrison refers to "radicalism," she advocates a move toward a socialist way of organizing society.

In liberation theology and in the pedagogy of Paulo Freire, there is also a strong emphasis on critical theory. Harrison appears to have received her inspiration from both of these sources. Since Harrison produced her work, feminist theoreticians have improved critical theory. Critical theory analyzes social problems, oppression, and economic injustice within the larger context of the public sphere. The theoretical underpinnings come from the social sciences and Marxist economics. Nancy Fraser writes: "To my mind, no one has yet improved on Marx's 1843 definition of critical theory as the 'self-clarification of the struggles and wishes of the age.'"[36]

The task of critical theory is to obtain the best analysis possible of an actual social problem. Feminist theory has provided an understanding of cultural and social exploitation and oppression, which has increased sensitivity toward exploited or oppressed groups.[37] How can feminist theory and critical theory together enable us to analyze economic injustice while recognizing groups whose basic needs have been neglected?

Although critical theory dates back to the time of Marx, in the twentieth century it started with the Frankfurt School in the 1930s and 1940s. Names like Max Horkheimer, Theodor Adorno, and Herbert Marcuse have brought fame and scholarly interest to the field. At present, Jürgen Habermas is a major figure in this tradition.

Critical theory is being revived in today's feminist theory discourse and surfaces now in communicative ethics through the work of Seyla Benhabib and in socialist-feminist theory through Nancy Fraser. Their view of critical theory is similar to that of Harrison, though each theorist addresses a different social problem.

Fraser uses critical theory and feminist theory to analyze the state of economics at the turn of the millennium.[38] She explains that the two main components of contemporary social change are the need for "recognition" and "redistribution." Recognition is the aim of many social movements seeking to remedy class oppression and exploitation. Fraser's rubric for redressing economic injustice is redistribution. Redistribution and recognition are hence the main themes for addressing economic and cultural injustice.[39] She asks, What would it take to make a politics of recognition support a politics of redistribution? She wants them to interact with each other (rather than compete) to provide a full explanatory framework for oppression and exploitation.[40]

Harrison uses radical social theory as a vehicle to approach political economy. She herself is a spokesperson for economic democracy. The confusion surrounding economic democracy and socialism is immense. Some claim that the former equals dictatorship by the proletariat.

For others, like Harrison, democracy is the essence of socialism. Harrison maintains that democracy demands democratic influence also in the economic arena.[41] In an economic democracy, decisions about money and property are made through the democratic process. Even those who do not own money and property will have a say in how taxes, common resources, and economic obligations will be handled. For Harrison, there can be no division between economics and politics. The two are intimately connected, and there are no existing political or economic systems that are separated within or from society. What she calls for is a new look at how they are connected and how political economy can be transformed. To achieve transformation, it is totally insufficient to investigate only the traditional four economic categories: laissez-faire capitalism, democratic-capitalist systems, democratic-socialist systems, and Marxist or communist systems.[42] For ethics in economics to be viable, the discipline needs to be fundamentally open in its views, both on economic systems and on democratic influence. For Harrison, the core of this debate is ideological.[43]

Contrary to Harrison, I maintain that, for analytical purposes, one can justify distinguishing between politics and economics. I am conscious that such a distinction is a complete construction and an academic exercise. Even so, it can bring greater clarity to the task of evaluating justice within economic theory and practice. It may turn out to be true that there is no ethic worthy of the name within this framework. But in order to accomplish change and to be true to critical theory, those reasons should be put forth. It could also be true that the "invisible hand" does indeed have an ethical component worth knowing.

Harrison on Ethics in Economics

Harrison does not call any existing economy a "Marxist economy," since none exhibits what Marx intended. In her view, Marx was a critic of existing social injustice rather than a builder of grand theories.[45] She judges this common misconception as a consequence of lack of historical scholarship. Marx's intention was to mount a critical analysis of economics and social problems of his time in a historical-materialistic manner.

A major trend among ethicists following in the steps of Niebuhr has been to focus elsewhere than economic democracy.[46] The need for moral approval of economic orders is constantly overridden by formal political rights. The task of ethics in economics, according to Harrison, is to "assess concretely the capacity of these systems to meet the physical needs of their people or evaluating their impact on the environment, other nations, or the longer term prospect of life on this planet."[46]

For serious scholars of economics, it is mandatory that they broaden their vision to include a thorough understanding of Marxism and social theory. Economic theory in a *chambre séparée* is not helpful for solving existing economic problems or for instigating social change that will lead to improved conditions for the poor.[47]

To create ethical economics, Harrison wants to utilize the larger body of radical social theory built on the Marxist tradition. No one fashion of political economy has emerged, but there is an intense debate about the need for urgent social change to solve the most obvious economic problems of today. Theologians need to integrate sound materialism into their thinking to avoid the persistent mind/body split. For feminists, this is an important insight, especially in the face of reactionary, even neofascist, Christianity that is increasingly common today. In a sense, physical labor and bread can be as spiritually reviving as prayer, Harrison suggests:

> A liaison between Christian theory and neo-Marxian political economy can deliver Christians from the strong lingering vestiges of an anti-materialist, world-denying spirituality that remains the complex legacy of Christianity's identification with male gender stereotypes and imperial political power. We also affirm that an adequate theological moral vision can deliver Marxists from the strong lingering vestiges of rationalistic scientism and cultural insensitivity. For feminist liberation theologians like myself, such mutual conversion is devoutly to be wished.[48]

Harrison wants to incorporate many facets of critical social theory into her economic analysis. She puts radical social theory ahead of sociology and neoclassical economic theory for four reasons.

The concreteness of radical theory is its first asset: it considers actual suffering and conflict. Radical social theory analyzes contradictions in the existing social order and political economy, with the goal of alleviating the oppression of the poor. In the footsteps of economists Adam Smith and David Ricardo, Marx was concerned about conflict in relation to economics. Conflict is not something that is constructed in Marxist theory—it is already and almost always already there. Marx was concerned with the origins of conflict and with developing strategies to mitigate the consequences in human suffering. Radical theory harbors a genuine concern for humane and democratic values. It does not claim to provide a fixed solution for every occasion; it must be flexible. Social laws are not static: social conflicts are changing, and hence a historical approach to conflict is better equipped to deal with and expect change. To have a fair knowledge of the causes of suffering and exploitation, a careful analysis of actual experience is necessary.

Second, radical theory assumes that it is possible to transform political economy. The capitalist mode of production, buying, and selling do not have the status of natural law. Any predetermined, static political economy is not in harmony with Christian ethics, nor is it consistent with historical knowledge about social change. The mode of production has changed in history, and it is rather safer to predict that change will continue to happen than to predict that it will not. From a Christian ethics perspective, it is imperative to operate in a manner that will end exploitation. This does not happen naturally within a capitalist system or any other system: it has to be argued for, decided upon, and acted on. Social change with positive consequences for the poor can occur and has occurred within capitalist systems. In fact, Marxists explicitly expected that capitalism would make adjustments needed to rectify blatant and potentially destabilizing economic injustice.[49]

The third advantage with radical social theory is that—in its connection to experience and change—it converges with Christian ethics. We can only assert moral reasoning in areas that are open to change. Radical theory favors a dialectical method—one that moves continually back and forth between a concrete situation and analysis of it—in exercising both social theory and political practice.

If economics were ruled by natural law—beyond our control—we could obviously not change anything. There is currently a consensus that economic theory and practice are social constructions—although there are people who think differently. Both radical social theory and most forms of

Christian ethics would assert that human community can transform practice so that a community can act as an agent against injustice. This option to act and transform plays a crucial role in Harrison's understanding of ethics, "to transform economic determinism."[50]

With the help of radical social theory, Harrison wants to gather information about the actual situation of oppression. Information about an oppressive situation must then be analyzed to find out what the underlying causes are and what can and needs to be rectified. To change what is wrong and to make improvements are fundamental in Harrison's thinking. What is also imperative in any ethical theory is that it end up in some kind of action. It is not enough to formulate the right analysis, to have the facts in hand, and to enlist on the side of the oppressed. Action must follow. In this way, empirical observations can be continually succeeded by a new analysis. This kind of hermeneutics is important to Harrison's view and shows her adherence to a dialectical method.

A fourth reason that Harrison commends radical theory in economics is that, in common with Christianity, it assumes that there is something universal about human nature and our way of relating to one another. This commonality is evident in our capacity for empathy—an important part of radical social theory, in Harrison's view. Through our ability to feel empathy, we can understand how economy is intertwined in the whole social fabric. All areas of social life have economic implications. Therefore, we cannot isolate human praxis from economic theory. To enable a holistic analysis of political economy, social theory and feminism both point to the interconnectedness of every part of human life, including its relations to economics. A simplistic ahistorical economic theory is not helpful to any analysis of public policy, or to altruism or solidarity.

Ethical norms are but one part of moral reasoning in liberation ethics. People's needs and combating injustice are complex issues, and simple norms are not sufficient to address them fully. The utilitarian focus on the greatest happiness for the largest number of people does not open the way to recognizing basic needs for those who are on the bottom, so utility also is insufficient for liberation theology or feminist liberation ethics.[51] There are many problems with utilitarian ethics—one is its lack of consideration for justice and its criteria of justice. Another one is the problem of who defines happiness or utility. Although there is no vision for genuine justice within utilitarianism, an advantage is its relative openness to including new views or specifications of utility.

Deontological ethics—the school of thought that derives ethical norms from "reason" and from "natural law"—does not suffice because of its previous oppressive history, heavy-laden with rigid rules applied to suppress people. Traditional deontology does not distinguish between how different situations affect people in different positions. Finally, deontology's reliance on pure reason feeds the mind/body split, which Harrison sees as one of the major faults with traditional patriarchal theory. Neglect of experience and real-life situations diminishes the analytical ability of deontological ethics.[52] But we should also note that Harrison's own stance on rules is ambiguous; though critical of rule-based ethics, she favors an ideology that puts the least first, without exception, as a basic rule. Although "the least" were not the priority of the old deontologists, hers is still a modified form of deontology.

Along with her advocacy of an economics informed by radical social theory, Harrison tries to root economics in a genuine commitment to justice. It is here that Harrison comes close to feminist interpretations of eighteenth-century philosopher David Hume. Harrison argues that *basic needs* are minimum conditions for liberation theologians speaking about what justice requires of normative ethics. Here again, Harrison refers to embodiment apparent in basic human needs such as dignity, food, shelter, health care, bodily integrity, nonalienating work, and cultural activity.[53] There is an inherent sense of utilitarianism in this approach, but that alone is not sufficient: concrete experience is necessary for moral reasoning.

Love and Justice

According to both Harrison and Niebuhr, the driving force behind the practice of justice is love. The fundamental basis for ethical commitment is love. Love is proclaimed as integral in the Christian tradition. The love of God as presented by the son of Mary and Joseph, the incarnated godhead, who loved the people around him at the price of his own life, is the foundation for justice.

Love is a sign of the divine. Practicing love is a way to acquire knowledge about God. Jesus is an example of empathy and solidarity with the oppressed. The traditional theological view on what is manifested in the death of Jesus is an interpretation that Harrison rebukes, and here she deviates from Niebuhr. Harrison interprets the death of Jesus as an act of love, not as a predetermined sacrificial death. He was one who did not cease the work of love and solidarity among his beloved people. The price for this love was his life.[54]

The school of Christian theology that has idealized love and made it into an exclusively spiritual relationship with God is not acceptable to Harrison. All aspects of our ability to love must be taken seriously; it is a divine gift, but only insofar as we put it to work. Love is foremost a relationship between people and must be embodied in real life. In this capacity, it bears witness to spiritual love. If embodied love is given priority, it will overcome the mind/body dichotomy that is prevalent in so much Christian theology. Any effort to separate love from corporeality is a heresy to Harrison. The embodiment of human spiritual and bodily knowledge is a result of feminist experience and reasoning. In love, we face our own vulnerability in a radical way.[55] This is what Harrison refers to when she speaks of embodied love. All people are in themselves signs of love or potential signs of love.

Only as we get acquainted with the depth of love will we know more about true spirituality and how it is integral to our lives. Love will enable us to live in right relationship with others. Right relationship is a crucial component of justice in Harrison's work, and here she refers to the work of Carter Heyward.[56] Right relationship is characterized as a will to improve the situation of the oppressed, to live in loving relationships with people around us, and to acknowledge that love must be practiced. Solidarity is the practice of love.[57] Right relationship is another criterion for love and justice. Embodied love and right relationship should be put into the information-analysis-action sequence that is required of feminist ethics. The practice of justice that Harrison calls for is grounded in "continuous relationship, fidelity to relationship, and mutual accountability."[58]

Women's moral theology is different from men's. Although Harrison doesn't detail this difference, she frequently refers to it. The position of women as women, which includes so much oppression, even in the developed world, is a social phenomenon, not something inherent in human nature. It has informed how women have developed a feminist ethics from personal experience of oppression.

What is fundamental to Christian feminist ethics? I find it hard to claim empathy as an exclusively Christian trait. While many ethicists disagree about what empathy really is, and feminists show a certain inclination toward David Hume's concept of sympathy, neither empathy nor sympathy is an exclusively Christian virtue. Harrison also included the concept of embodied love, which is physically expressed love beyond a mere feeling toward others.[59] Empathy, solidarity, and sympathy are virtues that Christians are expected to exhibit. In spite of these expectations, the virtue of sympathy is not especially evident in Christian institutions, countries, or peoples, although it is prominent in Christian teaching. It may be more correct to argue, along with Hume, that the *capability* of showing empathy, sympathy, and solidarity is inherent in every human person.[60] If it can be shown that these virtues are within human reach, feminist economists can argue that they be made equally applicable to the management of the global household.

Solidarity, however, seems fundamental to the Christian tradition, even if not an exclusively Christian trait, and it is mandated in Scripture: "Whatever you do to one of the least among you, you do to me" and "Love one another." In the Christian tradition, solidarity is love at work, and it knows no borders. In Jesus' preaching, love starts at the bottom, but no one is excluded. Therefore, both from a feminist ethical perspective and from the perspective of Christian ethics, the virtues of love and solidarity are supported.

Harrison's thinking is supported by other feminist theorists. In addition to the work of Nancy Fraser, Seyla Benhabib's thinking has helped shape the discipline. The notions of equality and respect in her "communicative ethics" have many similarities with Harrison's concept of right relationships. In the feminist communicative ethics advocated by Benhabib, the directive is to listen with mutual respect and true equality.[61] Equality is also basic to right relations in Harrison's work. Right relations cannot be based on binary and oppressive modes of reasoning. For equality to be effective, mutual recognition of equality is necessary. Everyone's story and everyone's reasons in regard to ethical judgment should be heard, regardless of their position, knowledge, experience, or power.

What Is Justice?

While maintaining particularity and contextuality within the economic sphere, it should be possible to describe what would constitute a move in the direction of economic justice. For Harrison, the issue is indeed involved; it has to do with the whole of human life. While this is hard to contradict, there are some features more directly concerned with economic life. To achieve economic justice and democracy, Harrison wants to involve both theory and practice and to acknowledge the complexity of the issues. In fact, it is here that Harrison's thinking comes together.

What is justice? Harrison chooses to relate the issue of justice to theology and, in particular, the ethical orientation of Jesus. The prime concern is for the disadvantaged, not for formal ethical method, when it comes to achieving justice. Harrison goes so far as to claim that while formal method may be correctly utilized in an ethical pursuit, oppression may still increase.

To her, this situation is unacceptable. Christian ethics was not formed simply for its own sake. Christian ethics must be concerned about content, about what happens to those in need. Harrison warns against the end result of an uncontrolled capitalist system: unbridled capitalism will destroy our planet and democracy as we know it. Her own position is clear: "Genuine, deep authentic economic democracy is an urgent need. Enabling people to understand this reality and to recover a capacity to long for economic justice as deeply as we desire political justice is the task of religious ethics today."[62]

Harrison's conclusion—to put justice before ethical method—appears obvious for many Christian theologians, albeit not for all. But those who agree with Harrison share the premise that there is a faith commitment to the poor and that this faith commitment is combined with empathy and solidarity. From that premise follows the conclusion to put the least first.[63]

Constantly watching what happens on the bottom as a way of developing criteria for how we manage our global household draws attention to the overwhelming evidence that grave material need or misery is a constant fact of life for many people. In some contexts and particular instances, like the ones Nancy Folbre has shown in her examples of collectives, a kind of empathy, sympathy, or solidarity spontaneously exists. But that in itself is not enough. It is a moral imperative for Christian ethics to strengthen the bases of life in community and to engender action for economic justice.

Where Spiritual Meets Material

The starting point for Harrison's ethical program is clarification of a conscious ideological position. She maintains, in no uncertain terms, that our stance in life—in science and in ethics—is heavily influenced by our ideological position. For herself, she maintains the perspectives of feminism, socialism, and Christianity, without ranking them in any order.

Three steps are required for the continual development of ethics. The first step must be to learn from social science. Knowledge is a prerequisite for relevant ethical work. Christian social ethics must continually be informed of the surrounding reality through the social sciences. The second is to analyze what we know and put it alongside our best understanding of what is just with the help of social-science and critical theory. From that work, we develop a position. Finally, the ethical task includes implementation of the achieved position since justice must be acted out. Until justice prevails, this part of our intellectual work is not done.

The foundation for Harrison's Christian ethics is the love shown by Jesus in the New Testament. He is firmly devoted to the people around him and to establishing justice among those he meets. He embodies love in his life and work. There is no division in this person: he encompasses all virtues and every person. Harrison denounced the traditional Christian emphasis on Jesus' painful, bloody sacrifice. Love is what Jesus proclaims, not sacrifice: love is a way to create just relations and an asset in the work for justice. Justice and love work together dialectically.

Harrison's strong emphasis on social and critical theory is a bridge to a feminist and secular theory and to a global discussion about ethics that is compatible with feminist communicative ethics. Christian ethics must not be confined to Christian circles but must embrace the concrete and specific situations of the world. So the material well-being of the least well off is crucial and cannot be divorced from spirituality. Matter and embodiment are linchpin ideas in her work. Traditional ways of splitting reality into spiritual and material realms are foreign to feminist ethics.

No economic system has ever successfully managed to provide for the well-being of all people in a meaningful, participatory, nonalienating, and nonoppressive way. Yet precisely those objectives are on Harrison's list of an ethical theory for economics.

Human nature is at the core of this failure, but Harrison argues that what is inherent in human nature is, above all, the capacity to love and to create right relations.

For Harrison, only limited injustice can be tolerated. Yet, at what point do considerations of justice enter economics? And is not justice a matter for individuals to carry, rather than for an academic theory or a large, impersonal economic system? Harrison does place responsibility on individuals, much like an obligation that applies to individuals within democratic systems. The decision to make life possible for all peoples is an ideological position that a person either shares or does not. But it is also a responsibility of economics itself. In dealing with both economic theory and practice, a limit to injustice is vital. Material well-being enables life, so that life may improve and become decent, and so that rights and respect and dignity may enter into the lives of people. Economics should be the foundational support of people's own abilities as free agents in their community.

6

A Feminist Approach
to Justice

We have noted the feminist critique of mainstream economics and the emergence of alternative perspectives in liberation theology and feminist ethics. Still, how can their considerations of economic and social justice come to the fore? This chapter constructs a theory of justice, building on narratives of injustice and the ethics of liberation theology. Biblical stories of justice and injustice and Christian social ethics provide the structure, with a focus on the work of ethicist Karen Lebacqz. Here also I begin to construct a feminist hermeneutics of justice with the help of previous material and also the work of theorist Iris Marion Young. Hermeneutics is a method used in much of the work conducted in feminist theology as well as liberation theology, and both Lebacqz and Harrison advocate a new hermeneutic.

Aiming for Justice

In her book *Six Theories of Justice,* Lebacqz presents three philosophical and three theological theories of justice produced by men. The major philosophical schools about justice are represented by utilitarian John Stuart Mill, contract theoretician John Rawls, and entitlement theoretician Robert Nozick. Lebacqz finds Rawls's priority of the disadvantaged appealing,[1] and Mill is significant as a founding father of utilitarianism.

Nozick receives attention in Lebacqz's work for his radical ideas. Lebacqz is respectful of his strong ideas about liberty but does not agree with his concepts of justice and private property.[2] Nozick's strong notion of entitlement does not take account of the countervailing ideas of rightful ownership and due process, such as were raised about historical acquisition of land in the United States.[3] The counterargument for this point is that if the land was forcefully taken from native populations, and if justice were to be restored, the land would be returned to their descendants. Although willing to modify their views to be relevant to changing times, radical neoliberals like Nozick maintain that no democratic decisions that impede personal freedom regarding private property can be just. Society has no right to decide about a person's property or make decisions to redistribute their property. The place of the state is simply as "the night-watch society," that is, a societal agency that protects the citizen's safety and private interests against perpetrators.[4] Nozick thus creates a total dichotomy between the private and the public sphere—and in the private sphere, democratic procedures no longer apply. As long as what we own is ours by right process, all is well.

This position accords well with how the ideology of private property was constructed by philosopher John Locke. He argued that property belongs rightfully to the person who has created value by adding labor or creativity to something that was not owned by anyone.[5] That this conception about right ownership still lives on is remarkable, since there is nothing left untouched by human hands or not owned by someone, and there is nowhere for a person to go who wants to create her own livelihood out of the commons.

Lebacqz's problem with both Rawls and Nozick is their starting point: a Kantian method of reasoning with no influence from practice. They both lack concern for what it would really mean to apply their scholarship to the history of the oppressed.[6] Rawls, Nozick, and Mills all approve of the market economy and the capitalist economic system.[7]

Lebacqz's theological material includes the United States Catholic bishops' 1986 letter on economic justice, Protestant theologian Reinhold Niebuhr, and Latin American liberation theologian José Miranda. The theological theories are critical of the capitalist system and concerned about how it affects the poor. Instead, they all seek distributive systems that will help the poor.[8] In contrast to these six visions, a feminist concept of justice employs *narrative*.

A Narrative Foundation of Justice

Narratives play an important role in all efforts to find meaning, and understanding narrative's role opens ways to enter the experience of others, understand their deepest values, and grasp injustice. Narrative can be a foundational resource for a feminist ethic of justice in three ways.

First, understanding another's story both presupposes and nurtures respect for the other. Universal dialogue is the objective that Seyla Benhabib emphasizes in communicative ethics, which includes gender as an integral factor.[9] Benhabib develops a procedure to pursue those problems.[10] But for her, the ability to put oneself in the place of "the concrete other" is a prerequisite to fruitful communication.[11] The norms for Benhabib's vision of interactive universal dialogue are universal moral respect and equality.[12]

Benhabib dismisses grand traditions, both religious and political. The time for grand traditions to dominate the interpretive position is over, she says.[13] Indeed, to critique the assumption that there exists a single grand narrative with universal authority is on target. In view of all that feminist theory has said about context and particularity, it is necessary to abolish aspirations for a single ideologically correct story for humankind.

Yet, we must also acknowledge, for dialogue to occur, there must be a common understanding of what is being discussed. This includes recognition that grand stories hold a vital position in many cultures. What cannot be assumed is a universal knowledge of culturally different stories. They have to be retold and explained in every new generation and to all new listeners. Any grand old story has many interpretations and can be plumbed anew for rich and deep insight into its cultural milieu.

Stories are thus fertile ground for conveying meaning. The complexity of understanding stories other than our own gives us a sense of the difficulty involved in any dialogue, let alone a global dialogue. If narratives are taken seriously, they hold valuable information about the "concrete other" and also about what it means to respect and treat the "other" as an equal. If our ambition is to include all interested parties in a global dialogue about justice, it is counterproductive to strip the dialogue of stories and experiences. In the Christian context, for instance, feminist theologians have always valued women's stories as a way to understand oppression. If this insight then interacts with feminist communicative ethics about dialogue, the tool kit will improve.

Second, in the analysis of injustice, biblical narratives are of major importance, especially for liberation theology. Christian tradition and theology grow out of a story, or rather many stories, that are collected in the Bible and given religious and ethical authority. The resources of the biblical tradition are rich and complex. Both those in power and those trying to obtain a better position in church or society have tried to demonstrate that they have God and the Bible on their side. The history of use and misuse of the Bible is in and of itself a huge topic, and feminist scholars like Rosemary Radford Ruether, Elizabeth Schüssler Fiorenza, Letty Russell, and Phyllis Trible have done extensive research on the misogynistic misuse of the Bible in the church. Accounts of how women have been subjugated within church, theology, and tradition are chilling and are now well known and often discussed in mainstream theology.

When Lebacqz wants to learn about justice, she begins with stories of injustice.[14] In the case of Scripture, she cites the Exodus event as the paramount experience of liberation from injustice.[15] A whole people was saved from oppression by supernatural intervention. The Jewish people learn of justice when they hear the Exodus story about how God intervened to liberate them from oppressors. The Exodus narrative provides an enduring image and a memory of justice.[16]

Borrowing from Fiorenza, Lebacqz calls recollection of such stories "biblical remembrance."[17] It entails reading the Bible from the perspective of the oppressed, with historical consciousness, and in light of the role of God in the Bible. For Lebacqz, God is justice and justice is God. One cannot be imagined without the other.[18]

A multitude of voices from personal experiences of oppression is represented in Lebacqz's *Justice in an Unjust World.* Here we find Nelle Morton's "hearing into speech" put into practice.[19] The need to tell one's story is taken seriously, and the process of telling it is used to overcome oppression.

Thus, third, telling of stories is a mode in which oppressed people can be recognized in their full human capacity. The weakness of the oppressed can be transformed into a position of strength, since understanding their experience underpins knowledge that can be used for change.[20] Both telling stories about oppression and transforming information into an intelligible narrative help establish a platform to fight injustice. Listening to stories from different people in different kinds of despair, the listeners inherit a memory—a shared remembrance of injustice—that will inform them of the many shapes and forms of injustice's disguise. We have stories from many quarters, from apartheid and slavery, and about violence, rape, genocide, homophobia, poverty, discrimination, and subjugation. Some of the stories are ancient and are found in Scripture, even in what are called "texts of terror."[21]

Lebacqz's use of narratives to illustrate justice within a Christian context connects her closely to liberation theology and shifts the focus of ethics to the oppressed as subjects in their own lives. Listening to the oppressed provides a new method to approach the issue of justice.[22] This method also includes a new way of using Scripture together with a Marxist method of political analysis.[23] Understanding justice through knowledge of injustice, Lebacqz claims, is an alternative to the grand theories of what constitutes justice.

Feminist Theory of Oppression

Telling stories about injustice is a way to improve knowledge about what justice may require. But what is injustice? Marxist analysis in liberation theology is insightful and places oppression in a context that aids understanding of exploitation of workers and poor people. Feminist theory, specifically the work of Iris Marion Young, is also helpful. Young sees five "faces" to oppression, domination, and their mechanisms.

The first "face" is exploitation of the power of work, which Young analyzes in a Marxist fashion. Young adds that exploitation involves not only class but also sex and race. This type of disempowerment was once generally well known and recognized. The issue of class has become muddled in the Western world, since most people are workers in one sense or other— they work for wages. Wages vary hugely, and working conditions also vary to such a degree that it makes no sense to say that all wage earners belong to the same class. And not all people who come from backgrounds other than European are exploited; nor are all women exploited. But it is still meaningful to refer to groups as exploited because of certain characteristics, mainly through economic hardships.[24] Exploitation is a phenomenon that Lebacqz also handles at length.[25] From farmworkers in South Africa to farmworkers in the United States, the story is the same: they are exploited. Or, as Lebacqz puts it, they are victims of "robbery."

The second face of oppression in Young's analysis is cultural marginalization. People are ousted from the mainstream of society because of something they lack: for example, the right education or the right contacts. Hence they are humiliated and disregarded, and they become economically vulnerable. People who live in the margin lack others' respect, equal options, and privacy.

The third factor in oppression is powerlessness, mainly political, among those who lack skills and professional standing or other pathways to influence. Young maintains that because of the knowledge obtained from how class structure functions, it is easier to understand how any type of oppression operates.[26] In Lebacqz's work, powerlessness is treated under the theme of repression, which is a more structured political way of keeping citizens outside of political decision-making.[27]

The fourth face of oppression is cultural imperialism, which makes people who do not belong to the dominant culture invisible. Invisibility is an effective way to subjugate people and to describe them in a manner they would not choose. It does not always result in economic deprivation in the way that labor exploitation, cultural marginalization, and political powerlessness do, but it is just as detrimental to self-respect and self-determination.[28]

Violence is the last face of oppression that Young accounts for. Violence, or the threat of it, is usually directed against women and minorities to keep them in place and fearful. It is the ultimate way to keep the oppressed in place, and it works in all cultures and in all social settings.

Images of Justice

The God of the Old Testament is Lebacqz's image of justice.[29] Just as there is a collective remembrance of injustice in the biblical stories, so there is a vision, a collective understanding of what God's justice means. First and foremost there is an experience or myth or story at the heart of longing for justice.

Lebacqz specifically invokes the example of Jesus. Jesus lives among the poor and blesses the poor. She asks if liberation and love of the poor are a sufficient description of justice and answers in the negative. Jesus joins the suffering poor and he is poor himself. But this, too, is not enough to describe justice. Curiously, she suggests that God's people are unable to understand God's justice.[30] Both Job's story and the Exodus story and, indeed, many of the miracles do not provide a picture of God's justice that can be analyzed by human logic.

Instead, God's justice may be best understood through its work in relationships. In the dispute with Job, God reestablishes a relationship with Job. Together, God and human beings work for justice. Human relationship with God is necessary to gain knowledge about God and to do justice in the way God intends. To know God is to know justice.[31] The right-relationship concept that was established by Carter Heyward and is used by Harrison also plays a part in Lebacqz's view of justice and of the relationship between love and justice.[32] To be liberated is to be freed on all levels, from oppressive social structures as well as from anything that inhibits right relationship with other human beings and God.

Noah's rainbow symbolizes justice and is an affirmation of the bond between God and God's people. It can be interpreted to mean that justice will never be fully achieved in our lifetimes; it is a promise for a distant future. But justice is a process of remembrance, love, and work; while human sensitivity to injustice reveals violations. This sensitivity is certainly greater among the victims of injustice. But the oppressors also have a role to play in submitting to the judgment of the justiceseekers.

Why a Feminist Hermeneutics of Justice?

A consistent request for new ways of understanding and forming a feminist theory of justice is expressed in the demand for a new hermeneutics. Hermeneutics is the theory of interpretation; it can be applied specifically to texts or more broadly to all conscious experience, including the experience of oppression or other injustice. Those who claim an "epistemological preference for the poor" as a hermeneutical key to injustice are often not specific in what they are referring to. To my knowledge, there are no arguments that claim that the poor have specific different ways of knowing or organizing knowledge. In some instances, the "preferential option for the poor" looks simply like a redressing of previous injustices.

It is not personal characteristics per se that are of interest to theorists; rather, it is personal experiences that serve as a focus for feminist liberation epistemology. And experience feeds knowledge. Lebacqz's thesis is that to understand the meaning of justice we need to listen to the experiences of those who are suffering from injustice. Yet it is not enough that the stories are told; the key point is what is learned about injustice from them.

As the study of methods of interpretation, hermeneutics belongs to the metalevel of theory. It asks, How do we understand and facilitate understanding? To argue that we have knowledge because of a particular experience tells us nothing about epistemology. It simply states an obvious social phenomenon. People have different kinds of knowledge, depending on their experience and training. We are also not sure about what is meant by experience.[33] Stories have acquired an important role in our efforts to understand experience, as is shown by, among others, Lebacqz.

Texts have traditionally been the subject matter of hermeneutics and they remain important. But there is a need to answer the call for an expanded or holistic hermeneutics so that a better and more encompassing understanding, in this case of justice, can be achieved. A major aim in Lebacqz's work is to acquire this knowledge and understanding from the perspective of the oppressed and from the experience of injustice. Social theory and critical theory are what Harrison asks to be included in Christian social ethics. Hermeneutics is, in essence, a method to improve understanding.[34] Feminist theory has given ample proof of the need for better understanding.

A hermeneutical circle—that is, a continually evolving relationship among a subject, an object, and understanding with a holistic foundation—is a social structure that will enable a return to the justice process any time there is a call for it. The outcome of this exercise will be a better understanding of what justice might mean in a particular situation. Likewise, a more all-encompassing hermeneutics may shed light on what justice requires. Some ideals are taken for granted, like equality, freedom, opportunity, and due process, though not without controversy. Harrison, for one, requires that solidarity, embodiment, right relations, basic human needs, and particularity be normative for justice. While Lebacqz's perspective is useful for understanding context, Harrison has much to contribute to improved ethical method. She comes to the task consistently with a set of norms and objectives that are recognizably hers and connects them to Christian theology, feminist theory, and critical theory.

When liberation ethicists refer to a preferential option for women or for the poor, it is an epistemological stance based on the assumption that the oppressed have a particular experience that is important to our understanding of injustice. But this epistemological claim does not refer to specific cognitive abilities of the oppressed. There are no essential differences between groups of people in their epistemological powers. Rather, the preferential option for the poor is an ideological position that accords with Christian feminist liberation ethics. Since I do not agree with Harrison that we need to position our whole investigation within an ideological framework, there are parts of reality that indeed must be accounted for, and the preferential option for the poor is such an instance. I am convinced that the poor have a right to express their experience of oppression, and their experience should be met with respect. How then can a claim of oppression be justified other than on the level of personal history? There is no simple answer to this question. It is ultimately important to acknowledge each individual's right to self-definition, but that may not be sufficient to dictate and inform actual work for social change.

Here the collective story is important. Inductive gathering of information is basic. Deductive methods do not work well with information that is taken at face value to inform feminist theory about the state of oppression. I do believe, for now at least, that we cannot utilize existing theories for our inductive thinking. This is a major methodological problem for feminist theory. Feminist theory needs much work in this area or it will be at a disadvantage in its theoretical project for years to come. I will not give up notion of "the personal is political." But how can one transform an idea like this to a theoretical level? Can feminist hermeneutics be a way to approach this methodological problem? For change to occur, there must be some method to apply.

What Is Justice?

We do not know enough about justice in theory and praxis. Justice seems to evade advanced efforts to define it. Lebacqz's suggestion that we learn about justice through injustice and the telling of stories of exploitation and oppression has many advantages, but it does not solve the problem of what constitutes justice. She does, however, present five principles that are crucial to justice: (1) Justice is a broad concept that draws on the richness of the biblical accounts of "right relationship." (2) Justice is not about rights but about responsibilities and duties. God's people are expected to care for one another. (3) Exploitation and oppression are at the heart of injustice; they distort "right relationship" for all involved. (4) Injustice rooted in exploitation and oppression requires a process of justice that will provide rescue/resistance and rebuke/reparations. "God's justice for the oppressed consists in liberation from oppression."(5) The forms of justice described are incomplete and partial. For a theory of justice to be acceptable, it must include its own possible fallacies, even though they may not yet be obvious.[35]

It seems plain that justice is, then, not a state of affairs but a continuous effort to overcome injustice. Justice is an ongoing process of diminishing injustice and establishing something more just. The notion of justice quickly takes on comparative notions—one condition is described as more or less just than another condition. The enterprise of establishing justice gets entangled with rational arguments for why one position is more just than another position. Different criteria are argued for or against. For example, is freedom more important to justice than equality? The philosophical ramifications of equality in relation to justice reach beyond anything that I try to solve. Instead, what I would like to do is to include narratives of injustice to improve and expand our understanding of justice; and both feminism and liberation theology help make that possible.

One role of theological justice is to maintain the utopian vision of justice. Justice remains a utopian vision because it cannot and will not fully overcome human errors, whether we call them sin or shortcomings. Nor are Christians better at justice than others.

A Global Dialogue

How can insights about justice be applied in a global context? As we have seen, Lebacqz insists on listening to stories, both biblical and contemporary, and her main effort in this listening is geared toward Christians. While this is worthwhile, it is not broad enough to support global feminist economics, an endeavor that encompasses a variety of faith expressions or is completely secular. While it is not sufficient to remain within the Christian context, it is not helpful to disregard it or any other context. While Lebacqz remains within a theological framework, Harrison connects to feminist theory in a larger context.

Feminist liberation ethics comes out of a Christian context and recognizes the need to be sensitive to other contexts, particularities, and preferences. Christianity is one religion that has some positive ethical connotations. But Christian culture is also culpable for a great many atrocities that have burdened the lives of people through the ages and still do today. Feminists of other religions, I am sure, pose many questions about their own contexts as well.

Ethicists looking for a more generalized or universal understanding of value have at least two options. The first is to decide on a single perspective of what justice is and then to subject others to one's standards. From the point of view of traditional patriarchal culture, this is a kind of status quo position. Patriarchal powers have not been required to justify themselves too often: hierarchy, dichotomy, and power over and against others are historically normative methods for Western Christian culture. In this culture, people can live in very oppressive situations over long periods of time and not even be aware of it.

Another option is to find a way to engage in dialogue with people of other persuasions about values. Benhabib, who stands in the tradition of critical theory with Jürgen Habermas, has put forth a version of feminist communicative ethics. As noted earlier, a key issue in communicative ethics is the equality of all people, their right to participate in the global dialogue, and respect for each person's equal value and mutuality in the process. Communicative ethics has fed feminist practice and been prevalent in the women's movement.

To participate in conversation with people of different persuasions requires respect for points of view drastically different from one's own, but above all for the persons who hold those views. Dialogue requires respect for the "concrete other." Respect must also be concrete to show that the other is a concrete person with the option to speak and be heard. A further inherent condition of any real dialogue is that there be a true chance that a change of views can happen. No one should be excluded from the ongoing conversation, and no voice should carry more weight than any other voice. Such dialogue is practical reasoning at its best that will help us shape the agenda and argue the case of those with no voice of their own. As this work progresses, it should be possible to see that people come from different contexts; they are particular but can still aim for universal understanding and commonalities in order for justice to increase. For progress in the process of justice to happen, it is necessary to maintain openness of mind and practice.

From Story to Theory

As Lebacqz so eloquently shows in *Six Theories of Justice,* considerable effort has gone into the project to establish criteria to define justice. The success is at best limited. Nor can it be said that feminist ethicists have themselves given any definitive description of justice. However, having rejected the grand theories of utilitarianism and deontology, Harrison and Lebacqz make points worth considering.

As Niebuhr argued, and Lebacqz maintains, justice is relative. Therefore, we must have ways to look at how relative, or even nonexistent, justice is. Women's stories and experiences are crucial in the search for a theory of justice. To listen to the oppressed is key to understanding the situation of oppression and discovering what oppression entails. Lebacqz makes listening to oppression her major, if not her only, method of obtaining information on the present situation. Harrison, by contrast, insists that theologians and ethicists also become more knowledgeable about social theory. Feminist ethicists must be observant about the situation at the bottom as well as about how oppressive relationships are structurally shaped and maintained. Perfect justice, when all good things are given to all people to the best of their utility, is highly unlikely to occur ever in this world. Yet this vision of perfect justice is an important one for human beings to hang on to.

Neither Lebacqz nor Harrison relies on the idea of essential differences regarding sex and gender. Harrison discusses how culture and history are important factors in gender roles, which have no ontological significance. She ponders the richness of biological sex, sexuality, femininity, masculinity, and chromosomes, and concludes that they are not essential for how men and women are morally significant actors. Both women and men can take on responsibility in the work for justice.

On the question of epistemology, both thinkers advocate a preferential option for the poor. I think it important to understand that this means that they favor the perspective of the oppressed and want to give preference to their perspective when it comes to distributive justice.

Following Niebuhr, Lebacqz qualifies justice and discusses degrees of justice and relative justice. Harrison emphasizes ideology as a value that needs to be included in order to have a critical consciousness. For both thinkers, freedom and equality are pivotal for justice. Freedom on the personal level has a high value for women. To be an agent of one's own life, to own property, to have a profession, and to enjoy democratic rights adds great value to life, in every way. This freedom is relatively new. As Bina Agarwal shows, there is very limited freedom even today in many women's lives. This lack of freedom pertains both to economic autonomy and to women's bodies.

From the perspective of feminist Christian ethics, equality is connected to the conviction that we are equally loved by God. We are all one creation, and we were all created for the same task: to love and to care for what is now and for what is to come. Equality is not something that we deserve in different measure according to some standard or norm. The overarching norm that requires equality is love.

Harrison is clear about the importance of provision of basic human needs as a minimum standard for a liberation ethics. This norm must be included in an ethics that will struggle for the oppressed.[36] Love of one's neighbor is a norm that grounds much of Christian ethics. This love is not a self-denying, sacrificial love, but a life-giving embodied version of the love of Jesus. Harrison does align herself with radical social theory founded in Marxist thought, and she sees the best available knowledge of social sciences as normative. Lebacqz remains inside the theological context but takes a firm position for the poor and the oppressed.

A feminist theory of justice should always be rooted in praxis. Subjects of analysis are always guided by some personal experience, and thus, experience is at the core of theoretical work. Stories about injustice tell us about shortcomings in the human community. The more blatant the stories, the clearer our understanding of unjust conditions. Feminist ethicists are concerned not so much about visions of perfect justice as about identifying, understanding, and redressing injustices. Women tend to be the most downtrodden among the exploited and are still expected to carry out enormous amounts of domestic and familial work. The struggle for justice begins here. The justice quest is, in sum, the effort to ensure that the oppressed and all interested people are given the option to live in right relations and are liberated from oppression.

PART THREE

ECONOMIC JUSTICE

7

BASIC HUMAN NEEDS:
A CRITERION FOR JUSTICE

In these final two chapters, I elaborate my own understanding of economic justice. To this end, I identify *basic human needs* as the first criterion of economic justice. I relate basic human needs to the insights of feminist liberation theology ethics developed in the preceding chapters. Basic needs is a concept that lends credence to the perspective of the poor and oppressed and takes their pressing problems seriously. My fundamental question is this: Can feminist liberation ethics strengthen the arguments for utilizing the concept of basic human needs in feminist economics? As we have seen, feminist liberation ethicists arrive at basic human needs through praxis—an outgrowth of liberation theology and Marxist theory and their understanding of the relationship between economic practice and theory. Provision for basic needs is crucial for liberation theology and a first step in the process of eliminating oppression, as seen in the work of several thinkers:

- In Beverly Harrison's view, no theory of justice that disregards basic needs has any validity.[1] When Karen Lebacqz discusses José Miranda's liberation theology, she presents his view that satisfaction of basic needs is not a sufficient aim for a theory of justice.[2]

- Bina Agarwal and Gita Sen focus on the poorest of women and the lack of consideration for women in the family and in the informal sector. The least affluent people in the world are women, and that is true around the globe.[3]

- Nancy Fraser discusses the issue of basic needs in relation to a U.S. welfare policy. To Fraser, *needs* denotes what most people use—commodities and services that she wants to have equally redistributed through political channels. In her case, the issue is only partially about sustaining life.[4] Fraser is representative of many feminist economists who deal with injustices within welfare-aspiring nations.

What would it mean if basic human needs were an organizing principle in economic theory and practice?

What Are Basic Human Needs?

The most common understanding of *basic human needs* is having consistent, reliable access to a sufficient supply of water, food, housing, elementary education, sanitation, and health care.[5]

This descriptive definition of human needs is instrumental in our search for a criterion that can be used to establish a norm for economic justice founded in "real life." Some needs are material, such as water, food, and housing. Some basic needs rely primarily on political decisions: education, health care, and sanitation are political or community responsibilities. We know that all those items vary from culture to culture, between women and men and children, and, therefore, we must always be sensitive to context.[6]

The common denominator is that basic human needs are similar for all people and they demand that a certain amount of resources be met. This understanding of needs coincides with the criteria presented by psychologist Abraham H. Maslow. According to Maslow, needs are basic if (1) their absence breeds illness, (2) their presence prevents illness, (3) their restoration cures illness, (4) under certain (complex) free-choice situations, meeting such needs is preferred by the deprived person over other satisfactions, and (5) they are found to be inactive, at a low ebb, or functionally absent in the healthy person.[7]

A number of basic needs are not included in this definition, as Maslow admits. If we view as needs what would provide reasonable human development in culture, religion, language, or other encompassing fields, other items might be considered basic. In some specific places, some provision for basic human needs has improved (for example, access to clean water has increased, and child mortality has decreased), but the overall global problems of providing them to all humans remain the same.[8]

There are no unified, global standards for when basic human needs are satisfied. The main objective is human survival, of course, guided by a rationale of the right to life.[9] The concept of sufficiency may vary between individuals. For example, calorie intake per day varies among women, children, and men. The amount of water needed varies in different geographical regions. But everybody needs food and water. Shelter needs are different in different situations. Some people prefer outdoor living, but even in the South Pacific, people live in some kind of shelter for protection from weather conditions.

Education is not the same everywhere, but it generally gives a person a chance to participate in culture and religion, and to know what is going on in the world. Also, for most careers, people need formal education. In other words, claiming that everybody has similar basic human needs does not necessarily mean that they are identical in every detail.

If we cannot measure or provide for needs according to a single standard of sufficiency, what is adequate? The concept of adequacy acknowledges the difference between people's needs and the quality of what they need. Every person needs the amount of food adequate for her; she also needs clean water, and she needs the education it takes for her to learn to manage in her particular social environment, as well as to read and write.

A factor recently added to the paradigm of basic human needs is sustainability. Derived from the work of environmentalists, sustainability is a condition that ranks high on lists of both physiological and psychological needs, and it may now be the modern counterpart to safety.[10] Especially for poor, rural populations, it is necessary to find ways to live that will not destroy the very resources they depend upon. Deforestation and soil erosion are two well-known threats to people, plants, and all nature. Two of the most vital problems for many women in poverty are availability of water and of fuel or energy for cooking. Both are often directly affected by environmental exploitation.[11] All efforts to provide for basic human needs must relate to local conditions and be adjusted to support them. No basic human needs can be sustained apart from the needs of nature. Ecologists are now looking at "the carrying capacity of the natural community or ecosystem."[12]

Provision for basic human needs should thus be defined as having an adequate and sufficient supply of water, food, shelter, basic education, basic health care, and sanitation in a sustainable manner.

Needs and Wants

Needs are often pictured as a pyramid. At the top of the pyramid, the fulfillment of all our needs and wants takes place. It is also on top of the pyramid that visions of perfect justice reign. The kingdom of God is such a vision of the perfect life, with perfect justice where the needs and wants and preferences of every one are satisfied. But what constitutes perfect fulfillment of human needs and wants?[13]

According to some theorists, self-actualization would be the perfect fulfillment of all needs and wants.[14] But the ideal of self-actualization itself comes from the privileged position of the white, Western middle class. For such a person, basic needs includes both needs and wants, that is, the entire pyramid that Maslow presented. In the minds of many privileged people, basic needs are provided by the welfare state. This all-encompassing notion of needs is clear in the way Fraser discusses needs in relation to the welfare state.[15]

Thus, it is important to differentiate needs from wants and preferences. In developed welfare societies like Sweden, the social expectation about needs that should be supplied by the state is vast, and is often referred to as "security from cradle to grave." Through high employment and high taxes, Swedish society has resources to provide for advanced health care, extensive parental leave, free education up to the doctoral level, good infrastructure, retirement pensions, and many generalized services. Though different in scale, the needs and wants discussed in this chapter exceed survival needs, but they are human needs that demand satisfaction. Some would claim that needs are equal to wants, but there is no end to human wants.[16] People often make good cases arguing that they need what they want. To make a clear distinction between the two, needs are roughly the same for all people. Needs must be met. Wants are wishes that people may have for all kind of things; they are individual in character. Wants might not be satisfied. For a full development of personal potential, there certainly are unlimited possibilities for the things, services, and conditions that may be required. When thinking about wants, an immanent notion of choice is involved. If I want toothpaste, I can certainly have the toothpaste of my preference, if I can afford toothpaste.

Basic human needs do not involve a lot of choice, even though a person may prefer rice to bread. There is nothing essentially different between affluent and poor people in the development of their needs and wants. As soon as the resources are available, people from very meager backgrounds do develop their level of needs and wants in the same way as those who were born into an affluent situation.

Global Community, Needs, and Economics

Basic human needs is a familiar concept among people concerned about poverty and development. Many economists have elaborated it, and it has reached a high level of acceptance in the international community.[17] During the 1970s, when the International Labor Organization (ILO) launched a major initiative to abolish poverty, the number of poor people on earth was estimated to be around 700 million.[18] Ironically enough, this focus on basic human needs by the global community has not helped to solve the actual problem: to make it possible for poor women and other poor people to provide for their basic needs. The challenge to eradicate poverty remains: and while the agreements in the global community to solve the problem are impressive, further help from economic theory itself is needed.

I am not looking at provision of basic human needs through channels of redistribution for people who cannot support themselves due to disabilities, age, infirmities, handicap, or the like: these cases are obviously tasks for redistribution. The quest is for able-bodied and otherwise able people to exercise their capabilities in order to provide for their own basic human needs. There are no places where such an exchange of work and money functions for everybody in any society; unemployment and underemployment are a plague even in rich countries. Political discussions about redistribution of wealth to meet human needs will continue. But this makes the question even more poignant: If the free-exchange market does not function under the best of circumstances, when does it work?

The market system works for many people, yet new people do come into the market exchange system at a steady rate, and that fact must be recognized and valued. There is also a steady stream of people on the exchange market who are forced out of work due to circumstances beyond their control. But from the point of view of the God of justice and love, and many who believe in this God, it is not enough that 3 billion or 4.5 billion people (out of more than 6 billion) can satisfy their basic needs. The crux of the matter is that those on the bottom are not capable of affecting or changing their own situation. A market marked by free exchange includes the notion of free movement, free entrance, and free exit from the market when competition functions well. Should this freedom not pertain to labor as well as capital?

In advanced theories about market equilibrium, basic assumptions tend to neglect the fact that many people lack the option to enter the market at all. There are, in fact, those who fall outside the supply-and-demand mechanism that creates market equilibrium and the right price. William D. A. Bryant discusses what is taught about market equilibrium and how the theorems "rest on general foundations when the opposite is arguably the case."[19] Bryant remarks that "the definition of market equilibrium usually requires that all individuals in the economy survive at equilibrium," yet "the survival of all agents is not an essential part of the definition of market equilibrium."[20]

Discussions about economic systems have not been central to the deliberations about providing aid or support to overcome the immediate hardships of the poor. The figures from the UN Social Summit in Copenhagen in 1995 estimated that as many as 1.2 billion people out of a world population then just below 6 billion lacked the means for creating a sufficient material livelihood. In 1999, the world population reached 6 billion people, and the World Bank's World Development Report increased the figure to 1.5 billion people surviving on less than a dollar a day. In 1976, the goal was to eliminate poverty among the then-estimated 700 million poor people by the year 2000. Assuming accuracy and integrity on the part of the global community, these statistics must be due to something more than political failure or inadequacy.[21] One suggestion from Nelson is that the neoclassical economic system is focusing on the wrong problems.

My focus is on the bottom of the pyramid of needs. My notion of basic human needs is intended to be instrumental in establishing a bottom line for economic justice. Thus, if economic theorists claim that they have a valid theory capable of providing for basic human needs in a sustainable manner, they will have established a theory that is situated within a process of justice. The search continues for such a theory and an economic practice that will give poor women and men a chance to provide for their own and their family's basic human needs in the market where free exchange of goods, work, and services happen. Part of the search is to test the existing market economy against the benchmark of basic human needs. As Nelson argues:

> An understanding of economics as centrally concerned with provisioning, or providing the necessaries of life, has implications quite different from the idea of economics as centrally concerned with exchange. In the exchange view, the primary distinguishing characteristic of a good is whether or not it can be exchanged on a market, not what human need or wants it may satisfy or what role it may play in a more global, ecological system.[22]

Nelson does not focus on the market; she either is focusing more on redistribution or has given up on the attempt to open up the market exchange to those on the bottom. In contrast, my investigation concerns exchange markets as they are portrayed in neoclassical economics.

Different Views on Human Needs

In *Management, Morality, and Man*, Göran Collste discusses human needs as a basis for his normative theory.[23] He makes a thorough review of Maslow's psychological theory regarding human needs. However, gender is not addressed in Collste's investigation; and since women so often are responsible for meeting basic needs of others, this is a shortcoming. Nor are physiological needs the focus for Collste: he is content to mention briefly such issues as the quality of food, drink, and air—things absolutely necessary for survival.[24] In his theory, basic needs are considered primary needs that must be satisfied first. He focuses his discussion instead on the needs for safety, community, self-respect, understanding and connection, self-fulfillment, and autonomy to support his normative theory, which reads in an abbreviated form as follows: (1) In cases where the gratification of the physiological needs of one or more persons is found to remain under a certain level, an alternative that would increase the physiological well-being of those concerned ought to be chosen; (2) When all individuals have reached x level, priority ought to be given to measures providing the necessary means of meeting the psychological and social needs of the individuals. Most of his work focuses on the latter objective.[25]

Without further discussion, the "x-level" subsistence level is taken as a given, which is explained by the fact that Collste addressed the situation in Sweden, a welfare state. It makes sense that a subsistence level is taken for granted, but it is also interesting to note the lack of arguments for basic needs, particularly economic arguments, since so many people's physiological needs are still not met, in Sweden and all over the world. Collste's work is an example of a justice theory that aims for perfect justice based on a theory of needs that doesn't adequately reflect reality. It is a theoretical construction, which he tests using democracy to influence demands in Swedish trade-union policy for economic justice.

Gratification of basic needs is too often taken to mean objects, things, possessions, money, clothes, automobiles, and the like. But these do not in themselves gratify the needs which, after basic needs are taken care of, Maslow defines as: (1) protection, safety, security; (2) membership in a family, a community, a clan, a gang, friendship, affection, love; (3) respect, self-esteem, approval, dignity, self-respect; and (4) freedom for the fullest development of one's talents and capacities, actualization of self.[26]

Maslow's list seems simple enough, yet there are so many people in the world who cannot even have their most obvious needs met. Because the lowest and most urgent needs are material, these tend to be generalized to a chiefly materialistic psychology of motivation, forgetting that there are higher, nonmaterial needs which are also "basic."[27] Above physiological needs, the pyramid has a layer of needs for safety and security. It is of great importance for people to feel secure and be ensured that their physiological needs will be met in a sustainable manner.

Maslow, too, pays little attention to physical needs. He mentions them as necessary and primary, without discussion. He moves quickly to more complicated needs. Maslow's neglect can be analyzed from a gender perspective: physiological needs are women's concern, nothing to discuss or worry about, and not worthy of theoretical analysis. From a feminist economic perspective, physiological needs are precisely where much of women's economic concerns are concentrated and where attention should be focused.

Justification for a Common Code of Needs

An extensive critique of the basic needs approach to development has been forthcoming from the countries that have been targeted for development aid. The basis of this critique is that the concept is too narrow and excludes important portions of what it takes to accomplish development. The shortcomings are particularly poignant with respect to human agency.[28] Their critique is similar to Gustavo Gutiérrez's—development is insensitive to human agency and, therefore, liberation is proposed as an all-encompassing objective. The reason I have limited my criterion to basic human needs is that universalization demands a certain simplification.

There are arguments against developing any kind of a common code for needs that apply universally to all human beings. Human diversity is so great that there are no grounds for any generalized claims about basic human needs, or any duty to provide for those needs. I have dealt with the issue of diversity with regard to basic human needs by recognizing difference in needs of calorie intake, water, shelter, education, healthcare, and sanitation. My main point, however, is the commonality of basic needs—there is no room for deviations; we share the same basic requirements for survival.

But then, the question as to who should answer to the claim for basic human needs is reasonable if they are to be valid globally. For any kind of basic human needs to be meaningfully advocated, there must be some agency or person to ask to fulfill them.[29] Although I have not committed myself to answer that question, I have raised the issue of the extent to which economics could be a vehicle to increase economic justice and facilitate meeting basic needs. The existence of some kind of global ethos around basic needs is shown by efforts made in the global community to ease pain, even though their success has been limited. And there are today no ways of globally enforcing a commitment to basic human needs; it is a voluntary undertaking by nations, voluntary organizations, churches, and international agencies.[30]

Freedom is important in the modern world, and any kind of definition of basic human needs making a claim for common human needs is immediately targeted for critique, since it imposes limits on human freedom to make voluntary choices. But there are limits to human uniqueness, and it is hard to understand why it would be important to defend individuality at the price of the lives of others. If everybody's basic needs were met, it would seem that commonness in regard to basic human needs, as a criterion, would be a cheap price to pay.

If the assumption is that a welfare society is required to provide for basic human needs, then there is a demand to share resources not voluntarily but through a system that will be forced on the individual. Individual autonomy is then limited since some resources are used for providing for common needs rather than private wants. Welfare states have taken on the responsibility to redistribute resources, and the effectiveness of their undertaking is reviewed regularly. Yet even welfare states do not manage completely to eradicate extreme poverty. This shortcoming tells us that there is something unjust happening also in welfare states, if there is agreement that justice requires access to basic human needs.

Human Agency

Feminist theory and the women's movement have developed crucial insights concerning women's individual agency or lack thereof. Feminist economists point out that women's abilities and rights must be considered if their needs are to be met.[31] Agarwal is concerned that the basic needs approach to development aimed at women tends to disregard the factors that initially disadvantaged women. If there is no coherent analysis on how women became poor in a disproportionate number, a basic need distribution for women is counterproductive.[32] She argues that poverty among women is caused by the lack of equal rights to land.

Amartya Sen has done tremendous work putting human capabilities on the map. It is a broad concept that includes human efforts in many fields, from the ability to survive on meager means to the ability to grasp complicated ideas. Access to some basic resources is not the goal but a means to the goal of actualizing human capabilities. He refers to the distinction made by Aristotle between the means and goals of human life. Basic assets are mere means.[33] The aim of public action must be to make it possible for people to use their capabilities. Capabilities refers to options to achieve certain levels of functioning.[34] Provision for basic human needs is but the first step on that road. Even though Sen has critiqued the scope of the focus on basic human needs, he does not deny the needs as such. The important point he makes is that a basic needs approach to development is insufficient and ineffective.

If the concept of basic needs in this work were supposed to suggest a criterion for development, it would indeed be insufficient, outdated, and insensitive to human agency and context. It is important to make the distinction between development work and attempts to improve a feminist theory of justice. These are different fields and demand different treatment. Justice is scrutinized from so many perspectives and has to withstand so much critical work that a certain simplicity in the criterion is excused. I maintain that basic human needs earns broad acceptance and is a code that almost anyone can understand.

Provision for basic human needs is instrumental in achieving the objective of the right to life. The right to life is a strong argument for increasing economic justice. To have a fair understanding of what is necessary to sustain livelihood is possible and facilitates generalization on a global scale.[35] Basic human needs clearly demonstrate what is adequate to meet the objective to maintain and sustain life on a global scale.[36]

A Criterion for Justice

A criterion to test justice in economics must at least be able to show the following: (1) that justice is improved if the criterion is implemented, (2) that it is universally applicable or argued successfully enough to qualify for a universal dialogue, and (3) that it can be checked in practice and can serve to build theory.

Why would satisfaction of basic human needs improve justice? People die every second from lack of provision for basic needs. Assurance of the right to life seems to be the ultimate basis for any kind of justice. Without livelihood, without life itself, there can be no form of justice. And the condition for sustenance of life is satisfaction of basic human needs in a sustainable manner. However, the right to life is not all. I have shown how the poor and oppressed are demanding to be able to satisfy their basic needs as a beginning of a process to achieve economic and social justice. That is why I have chosen to establish satisfaction of basic needs as a criterion for measuring how seriously economics and ethics consider the demands of the world's oppressed.

To be useful in a justice process, a criterion such as basic human needs must aim to be universal and hold up against almost all counterindications. Considering the flexibility that I have allowed for, it is difficult to defend the position that not all people are in need of minimal access to the items in this definition. The criterion of universality has been targeted for critique by social construction theorists, and I have tried to be cautious on this score by using only the most basic needs in my definition.

My intention is to use basic human needs as a measure and criterion that constitutes the bottom line of what is a minimum material condition for economic justice. In regard to justice, basic human needs is the litmus test that can be used universally. The items included in the criterion can all be tested, which is another important feature of a criterion.

One of the hardest questions to answer is this: Which arguments can constitute the right to life as a foundation for a minimum of justice? If life is to be sustained, basic human needs must be accessible, preferably by peoples' own capabilities. Right to life—that is, the right not to die prematurely—is recognized by the UN as a basic objective.[37] Christian dogma proclaims that all human beings are children of God, created by God, in the image and likeness of God. Since God embodies justice and love and wants what is best for humans, it is basic to assert that God desires for everyone to have the right to life. It is not a conditional right: it is a gift that is unmerited and distributed equally by the Just One. Ethicists from within the Christian tradition are unanimous in their support of the right to life. As to how this right shall be advocated in this world, there are any number of suggestions. One is that Christians, theologians, and ethicists advocate the right to life in the church and in the secular world.

From a feminist perspective, many reasons dictate why the right to life is foundational. Where the right to life is lacking, women are the primary victims. A fundamental aim for justice is to abolish oppression; to do so, ensuring basic needs to secure the right to life is a minimal requirement. The issue of justice has drawn a lot of attention in feminist moral theory. The philosophical question has been posed: What is a good criterion for justice? Feminists have come to the issue of justice from different perspectives. Beverly Harrison is adamant in insisting that justice is basic: "I believe that women have always been immersed in the struggle to create a flesh and blood community of love and justice, that we know much more of the radical work of love than does the dominant, otherworldly spirituality of Christianity."[38] And basic justice is the least to ask for. Her analysis is based on critical social theory and the real situation of the poor. That women have important insights to add is clear.

Karen Lebacqz approaches the issue of justice from the grass roots, and her focus is the epistemological privilege of the oppressed. The foundation for a justice process must always consider the poor first.[39] Lebacqz rejects the common ethical undertaking of discussing the different modes of just distribution without notice being taken of actual and real injustice: "It is the only honest place to begin."[40]

Clarification of women's conception of justice really took off in the care and justice debate of the early 1980s. Virginia Held made the point that moral theory reflects men's experiences in the public sphere, while the experiences of women are neglected. If there are differences in the experiences of women and men, these differences should be reflected. Until we know how this matter can be resolved, the obligation to consider the perspectives of both women and men remains.[41]

Psychologist Carol Gilligan came upon the notion of care while investigating women's sense of ethical dilemmas. She hypothesized that women's and men's moral development had different foundations. A woman's moral development is based on care and practical reasoning. In

Gilligan's understanding, care is an encompassing ethical judgment that will take into account the impact on other people when any decision is made. Men's moral development, by contrast, is based predominately on principled reasoning about justice.

Care rapidly became a core issue in discussions about justice in feminist theory. Care can be seen as a way to know the content and degree of justice, yet one can live with care without knowing about justice. However, according to Virginia Held, one cannot live without care. She states that there can be life without justice but not without care.[42] For this reason, she gives priority to care over justice, when and if they are set against one another.

Care is a necessity in order for human life to be sustained. How do we include it as a basic human need? Are there parts of care that are more vital to survival than others? Held discussed the notion of a "floor to justice," where injustice comes into the picture. In the same way, one could argue that there is a "floor to care" beneath which life will not prevail. In this argument, care certainly supports basic human needs as a criterion to evaluate justice and an instrument to protect the right to life.

When Seyla Benhabib analyzes the care and justice discussion, she situates justice within theorizing about the practice of care. Care is the content or domain, while justice is the theory. This makes it possible for Benhabib to maintain the deontological and universal character of moral theory.[43] By this move, Benhabib manages to combine care and justice as different concepts, but necessary parts of the larger moral discourse. It is also possible to maintain Held's priority for care if, as she postulates, a choice has to be made. Thus Gilligan's argument about moral development in personal lives does not collapse into two different concepts, but there is a relationship between them.

My understanding is that justice is a continuum from perfect to minimal justice and there must be criteria to evaluate where the justice process is going. There can be many different criteria within a justice process to assess the state of justice. In the case of basic human needs, criteria function to evaluate or measure justice in its own process.

Satisfying basic human needs could obviously be considered as a goal in itself. For many individuals in this world it is clearly a goal to achieve those basic needs, and that is fine. But for the theoretical endeavor to evaluate where justice is going, satisfaction of basic needs is only a means to a goal. Basic needs are a measure, a criterion for a larger enterprise—to provide a benchmark among others for a process toward economic justice. But one might also miss the justice process all together, for example, by not succeeding in making basic needs accessible.

So if it is so self-evident, why does it constitute an ethical problem? One important claim in this work lies in my insistence that ethical theory should have practical consequences, in this case for economics. Right to life is not granted to, and can by no means be relied on by, poor people. I suggest that the basic human needs concept be used as a criterion for how economics enters into the justice process. Basic human needs are basic requirements for sustaining life and can be used as a criterion in the global community to establish normative ethics for economics. An economic theory is viable for the provision of basic human needs if it gives poor people the option to provide for themselves in community. An economic system is viable in respect to basic human needs if it gives poor people the option to provide for themselves in community.

Measures of National Wealth and Welfare

Comparisons of basic human needs both within and between nations are difficult. To be accurate, the statistics must discriminate between basic welfare, needs, and gender. Welfare includes many more items than basic needs and, hence, is also more complicated. The way the global community has tried to compare need fulfillment between different peoples is influenced by statistics and economic measures.

As the need for an international comparison of wealth became obvious, a measure was established within the United Nations system, called the UN System of National Account (UNSNA). The initial work to establish the system was finalized in 1953. This system was built around the concept of gross national product (GNP).

GNP is a measure of domestic production of goods and services measured in money exchanged. The GNP measure was developed between the world wars since there was a need to assess countries as debtors in war. Among other things, the intention was to find a way to compare wealth between nations. Later, the need to compare countries arose to facilitate the operation of the International Monetary Fund and the World Bank.[44]

GNP is used to measure all exchanges involving money within a country. The critique directed to the GNP concerns its inefficiencies with regard to the informal sector, sustainable environment, foreign debt, reproductive work, natural resources, advertisements, natural catastrophes, accidents, and welfare.[45] Some of those items are not calculated into GNP; some, like reproductive work, add to welfare while others (like air pollution) exploit natural resources.[46] A minor adjustment has been made in recent years. Most countries now estimate gross domestic product (GDP), which does exclude money due to foreign investment and interest on national debts.[47]

When discrepancies between income and expenditure occur, it is called "statistical discrepancy."

It is very difficult to compare welfare using the GNP/GDP tool.[48] When the wealth of countries is compared using the median income per person per year, we get statistical information with little relevance for welfare. And even so, measurement among nations varies tremendously. The UNSNA is now in a process of change since it has been decided that the informal sector should be included and more attention should be paid to the gender variable.[49] The shortcomings of the GNP/GDP measures are widely acknowledged in regard to gender, and there is a steady stream of work going on to find other indices to measure production in economic terms and their effect in reducing poverty and protecting the environment.

Bruce E. Moon is a political economist who works with economic and statistical instruments to evaluate basic human needs.[50] He builds on earlier work at the Overseas Development Council by David Morris with the Physical Quality of Life Index (PQLI). Both are concerned about the lack of good measures and inadequacies in economics in development work. They pay homage to the GNP measure but are critical of its lack of capability for measuring what happens to the poor. A simple observation makes it clear that the median income measured by GNP (for example, GNP in the United States is the highest in the world) says nothing about the situation of the growing poor sector of the country. GNP is a measure that works for what it is intended for—to compare the wealth of countries with basically the same economic structure and industrial production.

When it comes to development or economic justice, one must seek other measurements.[51] The Physical Quality of Life Index consists of three variables assumed to provide tools for looking at the situation of the poor. They are as follows: (1) infant mortality, (2) life expectancy at the age of one year, and (3) literacy rates. The assumption is that those indications will mirror the sufficiency and adequacy of basic human needs. PQLI also offers the possibility of distinguishing between men and women.[52] Both Morris and Moon note that there isn't much theoretical foundation behind these tools, but they want to try them out in practice.[53]

A difficulty of measuring these variables has already been noted by Streeten et al. in their critique of Morris.[54] Morris's notions of PQLI met with general public approval; but Streeten et al. question if these three indicators, with little theoretical basis, could measure quality of life. Discussions abound about what different measures actually measure: such questions are hard to settle. However, the problem should be recognized and given due attention.

The global community needs to find tools that make it possible to find strategic ways and means for improving and determining the situation of the poor. Such concerns underlie the work of Herman Daly and John E. Cobb. They develop their own Index of Sustainable Economic Welfare (ISEW) mainly because of the lack of consideration for welfare, and for sustainability, in the PQLI.[55] Daly and Cobb suggest a total replacement of the GNP measure since it has a limited scope, disregards development, and cannot measure welfare. The PLQI works with the GNP measure, which Daly and Cobb critique. After all this time, the GNP still causes much confusion.

Since the 1990s, development of measures of welfare and poverty has taken place within the United Nations Development Program (UNDP) and these measures are recorded in its annual Human Development Report. UNDP's main indicator is the Human Development Index (HDI), which, like the PQLI, relies on three measures: (1) longevity, (2) literacy rates, and (3) GDP.[56] For this measure, data are available and comparisons between countries are possible.

UNDP is now also measuring or trying to measure gender differences. However, it is not known if it is a use or misuse of the term *gender* because there is no analysis of the construction of gender. What distinguishes the genders in those measures is biological sex, but there are other ways to measure gender. There are now two gender indices: Gender Development Index (GDI) and Gender Empowerment Measure (GEM). The GDI uses the same material as HDI but adjusts it for gender inequality. In no country is the GDI value greater than the HDI, which, in effect, means that the median for women is always lower than that for men.[57] GEM is a way of measuring women's participation in society and three variables are considered: (1) women's and men's percentage share of administrative and managerial positions, (2) their percentage share of professional and technical jobs, and (3) women's and men's percentage of parliamentary seats.

Furthermore, UNDP elaborates on the Capability Poverty Measure (CPM), which aims, first, to find out if people are well nourished. In order to measure nourishment, children under the age of five get weighed to see if they are malnourished. Second, CPM investigates access to healthy reproduction, which is counted in the number of births attended by trained staff. The third measure is women's literacy rate. Women's literacy has a direct effect on the social welfare of the family.[58] CPM is a complicated measure and data are even harder to obtain, but it gives witness to a clear ambition to find out more about what people can accomplish.

The PQLI has its strength in the fact that it actually concentrates on what happens to the poor. Improvement in different ways and kinds of measuring the human condition indicates that concern for how we might accomplish such development is growing. The number of measures developed does make it more difficult to make them operational to evaluate what is actually happening. It is not hard to guess that it will be hardest to estimate what happens on the bottom.

Women in Poverty

Women tend to end up well below average in all available statistics, with the exception of longevity. In the 1997 UNDP *Human Development Report,* the Gender Empowerment Measure (GEM) accounts for four measures intended to show the inclusion of women: seats in parliament, numbers in administrative and managerial jobs, numbers of teaching positions and technical positions, along with women's share of earned income. Women hold 12.9 percent of the parliamentary seats in the world. Women make up 14.1 percent of the administrative and managerial personnel. Among teachers and technical workers, women compose 39.3 percent, and women earn 30 percent of the wages in the world, while they earn 40 percent of the wages in the industrial world.[59]

Of all the births in the world, trained personnel attend 69 percent. The difference between the industrial world and developing countries is 99 percent to 63 percent, while the least developed countries have trained staff at only 29 percent of the births.

Of the children born live, 63 out of 1,000 die within the first year. In the industrial countries, 13 out of 1,000 die; and in the least developed countries, 110 out of 1,000 die within the first year. Of the children under five years of age, 31 percent globally are underweight, and also here the difference is great: 4 percent in the industrial world and 43 percent in the least developed countries are underweight.[60]

Since my intent is to improve arguments in order to facilitate change in what happens on the bottom of the economic scheme, women's situation is the obvious target to investigate. Statistics are important as indicators of the economic situation that women face. But there are many complications. Take women's share of earned wages in percentage terms. Women and men make up unequal numbers in the workforce. Many women work part-time. So what the statistics provide are indications of women's situation in the world. The indicators consistently show that women's situation is worse in the least developed countries.

It is remarkable that the United States has the highest ratio of poor women, compared to men, among the industrialized nations—more than 130 women to 100 men. The only industrialized country in the survey that has reversed this figure is Sweden, with 93 poor women to 100 poor men.[61] It was estimated that by the year 2000, almost all families under the poverty line in the United States would be headed by women.[62] This goes to show that the economic oppression of women is a universal phenomenon, although the numbers, the reasons, the contexts, and the particulars vary. According to every available criterion, statistics show that women lack the autonomy provided by having the sufficient means to fulfill basic human needs.

A grotesque example of how basic human needs affect other issues is female genital mutilation, which at first may look like an instance of cruel torture under the disguise of cultural habits.[63] One argument that is advocated in defense of mutilation, however, is that women or girl children who do not undergo this torturous procedure will not get married and they cannot provide for themselves outside marriage.[64]

Prostitution also figures in women's access to basic means. That the degrading occupation of prostitution is not a choice women freely make, but is a matter of survival, has been revealed by, among others, the Filipino feminist movement called Gabriella. They intervened not to stop prostitution but to make sure that the women got paid and kept up some hygiene standards!

The one thing on which women score higher than men in most cultures is longevity. No explanations are available to account for the fact that women live longer than men.[65] There are many clues as to why women live shorter lives in India—forced abortions, infanticide, food shortage, bride- or widow-burning.[66] It is not hard to conclude that, given the opportunity to provide basic human needs for themselves and their children, women would get out of a number of those situations.

Today there also exists a new trade—cheap female labor. Women are taken from their families and cultures to work in foreign countries as domestic servants, in sweatshops in free-trade zones, and as sex slaves. They send their meager income back to their country of origin, those countries increase their holdings of foreign currencies, and the families get a substantial contribution to their income. A clearer modern example of exploitation of labor is hard to come by.

To find ways to make the global, national, and local household function in a better way to provide for basic human needs in exchange for work, goods, and services would be a dramatic improvement in the situation and prospects of women around the globe.

Supporting Life

In this chapter I have presented basic human needs as a criterion and a minimal measure of economic justice. From feminist liberation ethics I have drawn material that demands that basic human needs be provided for if there is to be any justice at all. Feminist economists are eager to ask for provision for basic human needs when forming economic theory and practice.

Basic human needs are handled as a universal criterion applicable to all people. I have taken some care to distinguish between basic human needs and other needs, wants, and preferences. The minimal characteristics of basic human needs are stressed. The justification for basic human needs is that they are the same for everyone; they are not a matter of preference. There is a distinction between needs and wants that has to do exactly with the fact that basic needs are basic, while wants may be anything. Basic needs are also justified since they support the right to life as spelled out in international law and the global community through its agencies—not to mention in Christian and other religious traditions. Even considering the tremendous variety among peoples, there is a strong commonality in what it takes to sustain life: clean water, food, housing, basic education, basic healthcare, and sanitation. The insufficient provision for basic human needs is causing human suffering beyond comprehension and in higher measure to women and children in the global community.

Can the present system be changed so that able and willing persons can support themselves in at least a basic way? Can the market system approach economic justice in this minimal way? These questions are fundamental for a feminist theory of economic justice.

8

A FEMINIST THEORY
OF ECONOMIC JUSTICE

This work has investigated feminist critiques of neoclassical economics and what feminist liberation ethics might contribute to strengthening the assumptions of justice in feminist economics. We have seen that ethical assumptions have an important place in feminist economics and feminist theory. Is it possible to provide arguments from within feminist liberation theology and feminist ethics that will support the claims for justice made by feminist economists? I believe it is, and the business of this chapter is to frame those arguments. I have taken the ethical language prevalent in feminist economics to be a sign of concern for justice in the economic realm. Likewise, there is a parallel, explicit concern for economic justice that the feminist ethicists have articulated. The criterion that I have chosen to test aspirations to economic justice is how well economics as theory and practice can manage provision for meeting basic human needs. Accompanying this criterion, we will formulate some basic arguments, norms, and directions for a feminist theory of economic justice.

Economic justice is about just distribution of resources and services. There are two major ways to distribute resources and services. One is through redistribution—resources are acquired by an agent, state, or international body and then redistributed. This is how welfare states operate. There is a good deal of ethical work dealing with redistribution.[1] The other way to distribute goods and services is through market exchange. The main focus of neoclassical economics is what happens in the market. Enhancing the possibility for all interested and able people to access the

market in order to satisfy their basic needs is the focus of my work. This
chapter elaborates four themes to enhance the understanding of justice in
market economics, its theory and practice.

The first objective is to *strengthen the ethical arguments* that are used
by feminist economists. Feminist economists use ethical concepts like
rights and equality to support their critique and bolster their constructive
suggestions. In my opinion, those concepts and assumptions are too vague
to get at what is at the heart of the norms and values that feminist economists refer to. To focus instead on justice for the poor and to be specific
about equality and rights will make the arguments for justice stronger. The
"right relationship" concept from feminist liberation theology will help me
in establishing a foundation for equality.

The second objective is to *formulate normative elements* from feminist
liberation theology and its ethics for a more just economic theory and
practice. Which arguments are used to formulate a normative feminist liberation ethics for economic theory and practice? Where is such a normative ethics situated in the justice discourse? I will use work in the ethics of
feminist liberation theology to construct an ethics for economics starting
with the poor. My ambition is to try to find a feminist ethic that meets the
justice ambitions of feminist economics. The feminist ethicists that I have
investigated are eager to find ways to improve economic justice by (1) tak-
ing real social problems into account, (2) by listening to the stories of
injustice, and (3) by demanding liberation from oppression. To improve
the understanding of injustice and to create criteria for justice are ways of
introducing new checkpoints into a hermeneutics of justice.

The third theme is *the criterion of provision for basic human needs* as a
minimal level at which justice in economics can begin. I have argued that
the right to life is a recognized right in the global community, irrespective
of individual, collective, or national differences. Basic human needs are
instrumental in measuring how this objective is achieved. Without the
wherewithal to fulfill basic needs, the right to life is not respected. How
does this criterion work with concepts of equality, rights, liberation from
oppression, and right relations to improve justice in economics?

The final aim is to offer this work as a contribution to *an ongoing feminist dialogue about ethics and global economics.* The global economy raises
questions about ethical aims and principles far beyond the scope of this
work. We know that economic issues are often used ideologically, as an
excuse to brand others as enemies. One of the most infamous examples of
this in church history is the treatment that the Jewish people have suffered.
Economics is also a way to make scapegoats of people who lack sufficient
means for their livelihood. For example, the ethos in the United States
implies that everyone who is willing has it in his or her power to succeed,

and those who don't succeed have only themselves to blame. Economists, theologians, and ethicists of all creeds often find themselves in a position to reflect on deeds done in the past; but the urgent, present responsibility to address issues about women, injustice, and economics cannot be overemphasized. And how much more invigorating to look ahead!

A common feature among the scholars I have investigated is their concern for real-life problems. Julie Nelson, for example, wants to find an economic theory that, among other things, connects to the provision for basic needs and produces research with solid empirical material.[2] Bina Agarwal and Gita Sen have focused their research on how women fare in developing economies. Nancy Folbre is critical of how economic theory has perceived and presented people and the actual constraints that they face.[3] Karen Lebacqz explores injustice through people's stories to better understand what justice means.[4] Beverly Harrison is outspoken in her request for ethics to connect to real problems and critical theory.[5] Real social problems as the pinnacle of research corresponds with the strand of feminist theory that builds on critical theory as presented by Iris Young, Nancy Fraser, and Seyla Benhabib. The real-life problem of my work is that approximately 1.5 billion people lack access to provision for basic human needs, and that extreme poverty characterizes 1.5 billion more out of a total of 6 billion inhabitants on the globe.

Justice and Rights

It is important to distinguish between justice and rights. I have chosen to treat justice as a process, part of which is to establish standards for economics and to determine whether it can fulfill such basic requirements as provision for basic human needs. Access to basic human needs should take place primarily through people's free choice within the realm of economics. In contrast, justice is often spoken about in terms of criteria for just distribution. Should merits, skill, needs, or wants be the decisive indicator of how much should rightfully be distributed to each person? I have avoided this discussion and instead analyzed the problem from a single, different angle, focusing on those who barely survive.

Justice discourse takes on a different meaning if viewed from the perspective of the poor. Utilitarianism becomes obsolete because of its lack of concern for the poor.[6] At what point, we ask, does the economic status of the poor invalidate the economic systems that they are subject to? At what do they become simply unjust? I argue that if basic human needs cannot be provided for, preferably by individual agency, then there is no justice to discuss. The poor are facing absolute injustice in economic terms.

"Basic human needs" reflects not a single need but several: access to a sufficient supply of water, food, housing, elementary education, sanitation, and health care, all in a sustainable manner. So the implementation and evaluation of economic justice are also complex. To decide whether an economic system that that has managed to deliver only three of six basic needs is minimally just is a complex evaluative task. Obviously, people are better off with three basic needs being met than with none. But my inclination is to stay with the *whole concept* while being appreciative that the UNDP measures the variables involved separately.

Amartya Sen has been insistent that the basic human needs concept is insufficient. Instead, he has introduced the "capability" approach to human development.[7] I agree with him that this fuller measure would be desirable, at least where there actually exists a choice of functionings.[8] It is hard to imagine that people living on income of less than one dollar a day have much choice. This is not to say that people, and particularly women, have not given evidence of amazing capabilities to carve a living out of virtually nothing. How those capabilities noted by Sen could help to establish concrete economic claims for justice seems difficult to establish.

A more open-ended criterion, such as we have espoused, is more flexible, locally variable, and able to include different benchmarks to absorb new relevant information. It is a procedural justice approach that allows for flexibility, different premonitions, new information, old information, stories of injustice, standpoints, preferential option for the oppressed, and much more. When I argue for basic human needs as a fundamental criterion, I am asserting that justice has to start somewhere. The sky is the limit for the eventual achievement of justice, but lack of means to access even basic needs is simply unjust.

Rights are most often thought of as individual. They are often conceived as sets of freedoms that entitle a person to do certain things by her own will. Rights can also be claim rights, which entitle a person to have certain things. Both require a way to appeal for rights not granted. In Western democracies, the expectation is that rights are distributed equally. To have one's basic human needs satisfied is to have been granted the means for one's right to life, which is an internationally recognized fundamental human right.

Providing for basic human needs can happen in different ways. For example, as we saw in the last chapter, the Capability Poverty Measure (CPM) of the United National Development Program (UNDP), focuses on means through which basic needs may be met.[9] To exercise their right to life, people should have a right to improve their own situation, for example, by waged work or access to arable land. Microloans are a typical economic means to this goal. Microloans depend on women's capabilities to work within the existing economic system, as most of the borrowers are women. Another way of having one's basic needs met is through redistribution by the welfare state. Those who for various reasons cannot support themselves are taken care of by the community. Not many people live in these kinds of welfare states.

The cost to the global community of providing for basic needs is estimated by the UNDP at about $40 billion per year.[10] Combined military spending in the world amounts to about $800 billion per year.[11]

Justice as Right Relations

One important notion in the justice discourse of Lebacqz and Harrison is "right relations." Right relations are acknowledged by the fact that the peoples involved in a relationship recognize the relationship as just. The connotations of right relationship are personal rather than principled, but I am interested in the principles that lie behind the concept. Harrison opposes the commodification of relationship and maintains that right relations are at the center of moral discourse.[12] Right relations are marked by mutuality and respect.[13] Both Lebacqz and Harrison want to include love in their conceptions of justice, and here they connect to mainstream Christian ethics in the Niebuhr tradition.[14] Mutual equality and universal respect are themes that are also crucial to Seyla Benhabib's communicative ethics. Love is a theme that is not only found among ethicists; economists such as Julie Nelson and Nancy Folbre also refer to love when they discuss economic theory and then as a motivating force in people's actions and choices.

Right relations also include equality, a focus typical of feminist theory of all varieties. Feminist economists claim that equality before the law, equal rights, equal value, equal pay for equal work, and equal opportunity for women are ethical norms for economic theory and practice. The normative character of equality is increasingly being validated by all religions, by all democratic ideologies, and in all academic work irrespective of differences in ideologies. Feminists are at the forefront, advocating equality and at the same time affirming diversity, listening to experience, and respecting others on a global scale.[15] The feminist economists that I have reviewed tend to assume that equal value is self-evident value, though not realized.

On the theoretical level, there are few disagreements about equality in the international community. Equality of persons and of treatment under the law is an obvious right, according to international law, philosophical discourse, and political democracy. Yet for equality to be realized there must be some court of appeal. The nation-state has surfaced as the responsible, if not always reliable, body, and citizenship is a starting point for claiming that all citizens receive equal treatment.[16] Much feminist effort is put forth to support the UN and international laws, for example, in the slogan, "Women's rights are human rights."[17] To find a way to convey a global commonality about equality would solve a major problem for ethics, but at present there is no court of appeal that is accessible and effective beyond the nation-state.

There exists strong normative language agreed upon by all UN member states that speaks directly to the issue of equality. But there is no commonality in the foundation of those norms, and we are witnessing a growing resentment toward those conventions. One reason for this disagreement is precisely the problem of different philosophical foundations for jurisprudence, disregard for the importance of specific cultural contexts, and lack of consensus on the ways in which humans are essentially the same.[18]

Equal rights for women still need to be implemented. What is equality? One thing that equality does not connote is sameness of features, capabilities, and many other relevant human variables. This is an important point since issues of difference and sameness play a crucial role in feminist theory. Equality is required in many different ways not because we are all alike but in spite of the fact that we are all unique.[19] The aim for feminism is not to state sameness or difference as the basis for equality, but rather to fend for equality in practice. Some types of equality are necessary to obtain equality in economic matters: equality before the law, equal value, equal pay for equal work, and equal opportunity.

To find support for equality in economic theory is no easy thing. Equality is not an objective that neoclassical economic theory considers at length in the literature that I have studied. Criteria to decide matters of equality do not come spontaneously from within economic theory.

Universal claims are problematic, but equality represents a norm that has strong international support. Why is there agreement? Is the plea for equality a commonsense argument, something that we assume or take for granted because it has a prima facie quality? And if equality between women and men were a commonsense, prima facie norm, what might the reason be for that? The reasons for equality as feminist economists use them seem to build on an assumed intuitive and universal acceptance.[20]

"Equality of what?" is a question raised by Amartya Sen.[21] Equality seems easier to advocate in relation to specific topics. When it comes to equal distribution, it is clear that there are things that no one would find it valuable to distribute equally. Sen notes that there is no obvious need to distribute healthcare in equal measure, for example. Healthcare is better distributed to those who actually need it.[22] What are right relations in regard to equality and economics? Right relations represent a solid foundation for equality between the genders and between women and men, in the view of feminist ethics. "Equality of what" then becomes an issue: Who becomes equal, and who decides how equality is to be distributed?

One avenue for investigating human equality analyzes what it is that we value in the human person that sometimes results in equality. Feminist ethics provides the backbone for the full inquiry. The particular types of equality important to this work include equal rights before the law, equal opportunity, and equal wages.

Equal Value of Persons

"We are all one family, and it is our task in this new millennium to make ourselves and others aware of that—regardless of color—red or yellow or white or black—class, nationality, sex, lesbians, gays, and even straights—we are all one family," preached Desmond Tutu as he delivered a speech to an enthusiastic audience in a crowded auditorium at the University in Uppsala in April 2000.

The equal value of persons has a foundation in Christian theology, even though there are numerous instances in church history when equal value of persons has been negated or violated. Agreement in theory about the equal value of persons vanishes at the level of practice, and powers other than ethics and philosophy come into play.[23]

For Christian social ethics, equality has not been, and still is not, without problems. The most common Christian perversion of equal value is the idea that women and men have inescapably and divinely ordained different roles in the family, in the workplace, and in the Christian community, which assign them different values.[24] From a notion of essential difference, one can track how gender has been constructed in the Christian community, and gender roles assigned, albeit in slightly different manners in different strands of theology.

Yet Christian foundations for the equal value of persons can rest on creation: each person is created in the image of God. And there are numerous interpretations of what this likeness might mean. Is it through the capabilities (physical or mental skills) given to us in creation that we become equal? Obviously not, since we do have very different capabilities, and it would seem strange if they were the defining aspect of the image of God, particularly from the point of view of the godhead.

If we continue with the capability idea, that we are created so wonderfully because we resemble God, we have to account for an unresolved theodicy problem. If our different capabilities were the basis for our value, we would end up with a basis for inequality. Could it still be argued that God is just, if capabilities are distributed so arbitrarily?

In some way, God chooses to make us like Godself. For some ethicists, it is the capacity of human beings to distinguish between good and evil that is a presumed crucial likeness with God. Another foundation for equality in Christian ethics is the notion of each person as an object of the love of God as witnessed through Jesus. The love of God in Jesus is unqualified, bestowed on every person in equal measure regardless of merit. We are all equally loved without reference to our creed, race, sex, or sexual orientation, and each person can only be saved in her own right.

In the end, it seems plausible to assume that how the image of God is bestowed upon each person is something beyond our reason, something that one must either accept and respect or reject. It is in God's power, and is God's choice, to bestow equal value to all people.

Still, to say that a theory of equal value has a foundation in Christian social ethics is not to say that this foundation does not exist elsewhere. On the contrary, there is broad philosophical and humanistic understanding about the issue of equal value. The lack of equal value in real life is equally obvious. One way to remedy this is to offer different foundations for how equality is understood in different contexts. The conscientization that has developed in Christian quarters, for example, about equal value of people is in large measure due to the feminist critique of its neglect.

The Christian and humanistic conviction of the intrinsic value of persons is, in one way at least, contrary to how economic theory describes persons. In economic theory, labor is viewed in one basic aspect—as a cost. Costs are bad, costs should be kept down—unless, of course, investments in labor would increase profit. The less labor-intensive production becomes, the better. This disjuncture between Christian ethics and economic theory about the value of persons gives us an idea why Jesus said, "You cannot serve both God and Mammon." The underlying connotations of economics' valuing of people are at best exploitative. At worst, they are elitist and encourage hierarchical organization of work and society.

Equality before the Law

Bina Agarwal's work concentrates on women's land rights. Economic development of women in South Asia depends on their ability to exercise equal rights before the law in pursuing or litigating land issues.

If all human beings are assumed to be equal, including in legal matters, and everyone is treated equally, justice will improve. By and large, it has not thus far, and women in South Asia consider themselves to have a minimal chance of winning a legal claim against a husband, father, brother, or other male when it comes to land.

From a feminist perspective, this is one of the hard disjunctures between theory and practice. Constitutions, laws, and dogmas supporting equality but not implemented remain in the discretion of those in power. What good is international law if it does not change practice or, as Ghandi is quoted about Christianity, "What a good idea if it was tried"? The same critique is directed toward all the fine conventions, protocols, resolutions, codes and agreements, and international law created through the work of the UN and other international agencies, and accepted by nation-states. Even though the nation-states have been parties to the agreements, they seem to fall into oblivion.

Problems of implementing such agreements are enormous, and the courts of appeal are almost nonexistent or ineffective. There exists a committee in the UN that is organized to monitor the follow-through of the Convention on Elimination of All Forms of Discrimination against Women (CEDAW).[25] They meet once or twice every year and manage to do a good job, considering their resources. But the only power CEDAW has is to issue reprimands, thus giving countries a bad reputation—and that after enormous efforts with investigations and analysis. CEDAW cannot be approached by individuals who think they have a case in respect to the Convention. Agarwal provides the example of India, which fails to implement its own constitutional law regarding equality and thus prevents women from owning, controlling, and harvesting their own land.

Equal Opportunity

Women's quest for equal opportunity with men is global and ongoing. Women lack equal opportunity and access to education, jobs, food, political freedom, and agency. Of course, some equalized opportunities are not to be wished for: men run a greater risk of being killed by violent crimes, in accidents, and in war (although casualties in modern wars hit the civilian population to an overwhelming extent). Conversely, men lack some opportunities that women have greater access to, like child custody in the case of divorce.

Major areas of inequality that affect poor women's economic prospects are measured in UNDP's CPM (Capability Poverty Measure). It specifically tracks women's illiteracy, lack of access to professional staff at birth, and children's weight.[26] Women's limited access to literacy, natal care, and pediatric services deprives them of means to lead fulfilling lives. Literacy requires the opportunity to get an education, and there are large documented differences between girls and boys, women and men in this respect. Professional attendance at the time of giving birth is related to prenatal care, insurance or other means to afford healthcare, and information about availability of care. Female children tend to have lower weight than males, and there are several reasons for this, including lack of equal access to food. Rather than lack of monetary assets, the indicators reveal diminished potential for working within the existing economic system.

Women's unequal access to basic opportunities stems from many sources. Equal opportunity is a political, social, and ideological phenomenon and appears in many different shapes and forms. Because there are as many constructions as there are societies, religions, and cultures, inequalities are due to human diversity, kinship, race, sex, class, different health conditions, unique brains, ages, and sexual orientations. In relation to basic human needs, equal opportunities would mean for everyone freely to exercise their capabilities (within the limits of the law) to satisfy their basic needs within existing economic systems.

Amartya Sen explores the notion of capabilities as a personal trait that distinguishes one person from the next. He builds on individualistic virtue ethics rooted in Aristotelian thinking.[27] One stronghold of capabilities from a feminist point of view is its recognition of each person as unique, not to be mixed up in large categories that ignore important capabilities and differences. Yet, stress on capabilities does not lead to opportunity, since one of Sen's main points is to focus on the individual to find what she can accomplish that is beyond distribution and measurements. While there is no such thing as equal capabilities, equal opportunity as a spur to developing capabilities should be taken seriously as a way to enhance people's living conditions. Another case for equal opportunity is the chance to influence the quality of collective or democratic decision making in one's own context—socially, politically, and economically. Many argue that for economic systems to work well, democracy needs to be enhanced. And if the economy works well, there is an enhanced possibility that society may acquire more resources to redistribute. Generally speaking, women have less access to education, to political and social influence, and to monetary resources with which to influence decisions.[28] If women were given equal opportunity, the consequences for a world that is challenged to erase poverty can only be imagined. Many competent women do not get a chance to do their best because of the lack of equal opportunity. In economic terms, this is irrational and inefficient.

Equal Pay for Equal Work

Lack of equal pay for equal work is one example of women's deprivation of opportunities, and it is an old theme. All feminist economists, not to say all economists, are well aware of the gap between women and men when the paycheck arrives. Neoclassical economists provide ample reasons for this: women are mothers, are married, give birth, have fewer muscles, do not have to be the primary support for their family, and have generally less work experience and lower education than men. At one time, the reason for paying women less was to dissuade them from crowding the labor market.[29] This discrepancy pervades all sections of the world's economies—every country and every occupation—and provides an excellent criterion for measuring inequality.[30] The situation is well documented in reliable statistics.

From an ethical point of view, very few people advocate for this discrepancy and even fewer arguments exist to justify it. Even so, a short look in the rearview mirror provides one good example of how the inequity has been maintained, and that is the demand for a "family wage." Men support families and hence they need and are justified in asking for and receiving a higher salary.

How women were denied access to the labor market provides another example. Women were not allowed access to certain training and certain jobs.[31] Of course, those jobs were better paid. The arguments to keep women out of the labor market are old, but the problems with unequal salaries remain without support or justification from either ethics or economics. As I showed in chapter 7, there have been efforts to argue for the discrepancy, albeit not very strong or successful. Here is a case where there is a great deal of agreement, perhaps even consensus, that the objective, yet well-reasoned arguments for equal pay do not result in implementation of equal pay.

The lack of equal pay for equal work is also an inconsistency in economic theory, which maintains that if there is cheaper comparable labor available for hire, it will be hired in a free-market economy. If that were so, fields or occupations where women work at lower wages would be dominated by women, plainly not the case. Economic theory cannot explain the unequal pay problem within its own parameters. Economist Barbara Bergmann puts the cause of wage discrepancy squarely in the lap of patriarchy and shows how sexism and racism work independently of the usual dictates of marginal productivity analysis.[32]

Justice as Liberation from Oppression

To understand justice, we should start with knowing, seeing, and listening to stories about injustice. Real people with real experiences and those with knowledge from the social sciences demand inclusion. Justice as liberation is more complex than distribution of resources or fulfillment of basic needs. Justice as liberation must also resolve or dissolve oppressive barriers, such as discrimination and domination.[33] Justice is liberation from poverty but also from oppressive measures that infringe on other personal and communal liberties.

Theorists differ about the roots and measures of infringements on personal agency. According to Nancy Folbre, they are constraints on the different groups we belong to and the assets we command. According to

Nelson, they are consistent negative valuation of feminine characteristics. In Harrison's view, constraints on women are rooted in deficient insights of disembodied theology. According to Lebacqz, their roots lie in faulty conceptions of injustice. For Agarwal, they stem from neglect of women's legal rights affecting their economic self-sufficiency. For Gita Sen, disregard for women's equality in development economics is to blame. These theorists present the multiplicity of ways in which women are oppressed. Some factors pertain to basic needs and some to ideal needs. Both material and ideal needs are embraced by a feminist justice ethics, but in this work I concentrate on material needs, on how to obtain the resources necessary to satisfy basic needs.

White, educated, well-to-do church people living in the Northern and Western Hemispheres are privileged to an extent that is hard even for our own grandparents to grasp. Even so, many such people have personally experienced or been touched by hardship. In this way, their ability to identify with people who are severely oppressed is increased. The 70 percent of the world's poor, well above 1 billion people, who are women and children is our focus, as is their destiny.[34] Their experience of oppression is not written in one book but in countless stories. One oppressed woman told me the story of her life. She was a farmworker and mother of twelve children. Because there was never enough food, clothes, education, or healthcare, in her mind it was God's mercy that saw them grow up to be adults. She was my grandmother. All women and children who live a life framed by injustice have a story to tell. The globe is filled with injustice; the nation-state is not a place where people live a life in justice, nor is the family, nor, for that matter, is the church. The main course of events that has influenced liberation feminist ethics' claim for justice is experience of injustice. For the poor and oppressed women of the world, basic liberation from oppression would mean a chance to manage fulfillment of their own basic needs. It seems impossible to give up this position with regard to justice. The fact that the ongoing suffering of many poor people has been given such insufficient attention in Christian ethics, especially as it pertains to economics, is partially due to what Harrison has pointed out as a certain lethargy among ethicists to face up to the basic questions of community.

Justice discourse is diverse and populated by many actors: theologians, politicians, philosophers, idealists, and lawyers. Lack of consensus about what constitutes justice remains a most striking feature in the global community. The liberal tradition discusses justice in terms of distribution, while feminist critical theory tends to be more encompassing and includes issues of marginalization, exploitation, violence, and disempowerment. The justice process starts with recognition of injustice, while actual experience fuels the process of gaining or restoring justice. Data from the social sciences that are congruent with experience of injustice are helpful for our analysis. Indeed, knowledge about injustice has increased: international bodies now know and measure how much people eat, the difference in calorie intake between women and men and between male and female children, the per capita income of people, the fortunes in the world. There are measures of access to clean water, healthcare, and the number of children and adults who are illiterate. The deficiencies of measures of women's work in the formal and informal sector are now being addressed.[35] Although particulars differ, the demand for liberation from oppression, concentrating on concrete gauges of equality and provision for basic needs, is univocal among feminist theoreticians, economists, and ethicists.

Feminist Liberation Ethics

What good can a Christian feminist ethics do? If those of the Christian faith or tradition wish to communicate with others on issues of economic justice, we must see our own context as just that. North Atlantic Christianity is one context from which some who call themselves Christians have come to understand and be in solidarity with the poor. In the Christian fold, many of these people come from the South and provide eye-opening reflections on injustice. Others claim other contexts, reasons, and metaphors that have informed their solidarity. Alleviating poverty seems to be a common concern among feminist theoreticians and feminist ethicists from a variety of contexts. That is why I use crude materialism as the measure of justice: provision for basic human needs is a concept that can be understood universally. Poverty is universally acknowledged and addressed. It has an explicit urgency, particularly the plight of people who lack provision for basic needs. For justice in economics, it is the obvious problem to address.

When it comes to economic justice, Harrison allies with critical theory. She connects critical theory's insights about economic justice to Christian love. Love and justice work together in a dialectical manner so that both are enlarged. This conjunction is closely paralleled by liberation theology and its materialist ideology. Christian social ethics is mandated to attend to economics, both as political economy and as market economy, to find out what enhances human community and what exploits it.

What are the good arguments to uphold basic needs from a feminist liberation ethics point of view? Women who have experienced utter despair over lack of resources to meet basic needs are lifted up in respect and esteem in the biblical accounts. The biblical stories anchor the ethical mandate to help the poor in the very word of God, who promises to deliver them from their travail.

Biblical stories are cherished and used as encouraging examples. When widows and fatherless children were fed, Israel received divine approval. Even when Adam and Eve were forced out of paradise, their basic needs were addressed: "With labor you shall win your food from it all the days of your life. It will grow thorns and thistles for you, none but wild plants for you to eat. You shall gain your bread by the sweat of your brow until you return to the ground" (Genesis 3:18-19). And, of course, in the New Testament Jesus taught his disciples to pray for daily bread.

Jesus scolded his disciples because they thought that the oil that a woman used on his body was wasted, saying, "You have the poor among you always" (Matthew 26:11). If this is a prophecy of the state of affairs in times to come, we can indeed confirm that he was right. But what if his was more a reflection about human greed? The means to change the course of events is available. This is what many Christian ethicists are asking, feminist ethicists among them.

Why feminist liberation ethics? As we have seen, there is congruence among the works of the feminists that I have examined. Feminist theory, of the type portrayed in critical theory, raises many of the same issues in regard to justice as do feminist ethicists. Likewise, feminist economists are concerned about justice issues within economics that relate to women. Feminist liberation ethics presents encompassing theories of justice and focuses on the most disadvantaged. Feminist liberation ethics gives attention to particular factors, especially those pertaining to the oppression of women, that previously were not noticed nor addressed.

Basic Human Needs as a Criterion of Justice

Employing the criterion of providing for basic human needs will help to inject a standard of justice in the theory and practice of economics. I maintain that we need criteria for economic justice with the broadest possible support, such as can be found for basic human needs. There is a considerable collective self-interest to such a rule. The interconnectedness of the human community on a global scale is well established, as witnessed by Daly and Cobb in *For the Common Good*, and by Archbishop Desmond Tutu as well as Harrison, Lebacqz, Agarwal, Folbre, Nelson, and Gita Sen.

I also believe that most people have an intuitive desire for the well-being of others. The present onslaught of theories of justice relies on such an intuitive recognition of the plight of the poor—tomorrow it might be me or my loved ones. Most people do not know who their neighbors will be in just a generation or what nationality or economic status their grandchildren will have. To support every human being's capability to make a living is a claim to justice that corresponds to reason and sound self-interest.

But why should basic human needs be given priority ahead of, for example, common business ethics? Obviously, there are a number of other situations when the market economy demands and works under rules of ethics. Yet the main objective of ethical rules in economics seems to be to create a reliable environment for doing business—not to improve justice.[36] That economics deals with ethics does not mean that it deals with justice.

The provision for basic human needs is a generalized, universal goal and provides a concrete yet flexible measure to improve justice. As a criterion, it is applicable to different strands of equality: it improves right relations, and it is a means of diminishing oppression.

A Feminist Hermeneutics of Justice

As we have seen, Karen Lebacqz focuses her investigation on stories about injustice and insists that a theory of justice must start there. She calls for a new hermeneutics, a new way of interpreting ethical situations. Stories of injustice, the biblical legacy, and historical consciousness form the basis for her method for assessing the demands of justice in a given situation.

Establishing a bottom line for justice in economics is one objective of this work. But what distinguishes justice from injustice in economics? My thesis is that justice at a minimal level within the economic realm demands that all able and interested people have the option, within the existing economic system, to provide for their basic human needs. If such an economic system were developed, it would provide most people with a safe and stable framework for planning and living their lives, utilizing their abilities, and choosing their preferred livelihood.

Lebacqz's and Harrison's proposals for hermeneutics help us assess and implement the idea I propose. The hermeneutical modus operandi allows for continuous input of new information, in a number of forms—from feminist theorists in the field of ethics and economics to theologians and the poor themselves. Feminist liberation ethics understands right and wrong as continuously subject to evaluation by those who suffer from injustice. The feminist "hermeneutical circle" is thus an open-ended spiral. At its best, the stage is not permanently set: the program will always be open to new actors and new information. This hermeneutical spiral can change when new people, new problems, and new information are included. The feminist liberation ethical assumption is that the spiral will first determine whether basic needs are accessible. The justice process includes some concrete measures, such as those we have included in the basic human needs criterion. The data may or may not coincide with stories of injustice that provide a different, less quantifiable measure based on personal experience. If the stories coincide with available data, it will strengthen the interpretation. If they do not coincide, the proposal about basic human needs is weakened.

The ethical qualifier that is used most often among feminist economists is equality. It can augment or illuminate our proposal about basic human needs. Equality has many aspects within economics, education, and law. Equality of wages is one measurable variable, and several instances of equality before the law and equal opportunity can also be measured and included in the hermeneutical circle.

Other kinds of data are harder to include, for example, those concerning right relations. How can mutual respect and universal equality and love be measured and included in a justice process in this hermeneutical circle? Those are typically *ideal* variables that ethicists from many perspectives endorse in their work. It would at least simplify understanding if those ideal variables were kept apart from the more material ones that can be measured in practice, such as many of the aspects of equality. At times, the ideal variables are intertwined with the material ones and can probably be used in both ideal and material types of hermeneutics.

Issues regarding equal value, rights, and opportunity are benchmarks to be added to a feminist justice hermeneutics concerning economics. Most of the measures tend to coincide with Iris Marion Young's five faces of oppression and Nancy Fraser´s accounts of recognition and redistribution. The benchmarks give witness to how well right relationships or other ideal variables are realized. For example, a feminist hermeneutic for minimal economic justice must:

- Safeguard provision of basic needs through existing economic systems
- Keep track of what happens to the poor through social sciences
- Follow existing measures of poverty
- Improve women's position on the equality variables
- Follow how women fare in deliberations before the law
- Seek out stories of injustice and learn from them
- Constantly attend to the aim of alleviating poverty

Feminist ethics are in the forefront of some of those items, like women's equality and listening to stories of injustice. Among the ideal measures, most are deliberated through feminist theory and ethics, and they include:

- Liberation from oppression
- Right relations and embodiment
- Mutuality and respect
- Universal egalitarianism

For a feminist hermeneutics for minimal economic justice, the key question asked in economics and in a hermeneutics of suspicion is this: Who profits from this? Will the proposed measures improve or worsen the plight of the poor?

Most things that happen in the economic arena have little effect on the poor, but extreme exploitation is a rampant contemporary phenomenon that needs careful examination. One might well ask: What is worse, being exploited and losing one's health, or being without a job and outside the frame of exploitation?

The biblical legacy and social and historical knowledge are what liberation theology brings to the understanding of those phenomena. Critical theory makes the observer aware of what happens in exploitative schemes. Liberation from oppression is a measure of justice that is not identical with economic justice, but it has a great effect on people's freedom and capabilities all the same. A richer, more complex, and more transparent understanding of what goes into the interpretation of economic justice, such as we have proposed here, will make the case for women's requests for improvement stronger.

Finally, if economic justice is to be improved, the democratic idea of letting people participate in deciding issues that concern them needs to be more widely practiced. Democratic economic systems are key, if we are interested in a form of justice that encompasses economics.[37]

Transforming Economics—and People's Lives

In this work I have shown how feminist economists and ethicists share issues pertaining to economic justice, a common and important feature in their work. The issue of justice in economics is seen both as a distributive task for community and as a problem that deserves closer attention, in its scientific or theoretical side as well as in its actual market face. What if the task of satisfying all people's basic needs were the organizing center of economic research? How would it be possible to open up the market economy to make it possible for all able and willing persons to provide for their basic needs? Those are enormous questions, but feminists in ethics and economics are courageous enough to raise them. About 1.5 billion people await the answers.

Feminist economists and ethicists share analytical perspectives; they give special attention to the perspective of women, who are at a disadvantage in access to resources or distribution of resources. Feminist ethicists and economists also share concerns about justice and women's oppression. Solutions to the issues brought to the fore by feminist economists and ethicists are of crucial importance for ethical pursuit in the global community.

We have seen that gender plays a decisive role in the neglect of the individual in neoclassical economic theory. Gender is unaccounted for in the way neoclassical economics reduces human beings to rational and narrowly self-interested beings. An ethics of economic justice will require that the traditional view in economics about self-interest be broadened. There is something to be said for sound self-interest, when the self is understood collectively or relationally.[38] No one (not even a man) is an island. We are in this together—all 6 billion of us. Narrow self-interest pays attention only to atomistic views of the individual. Human beings are interdependent, and we do not even know the full extent to which we are intertwined.

On many scores, biological sex can be sufficient to find measures of injustice on a global scale. Yet the routine use of gender in much of UNDP statistics may render the concept useless for the complicated analysis of particular constructions of gender as exhibited in today's complex and diverse social contexts. But the subject is complicated, and theory must always adhere to particularities, perhaps with the help of Nelson's gender-value compass.

Feminist economists tend to have a holistic approach when designing and doing research. Information from the social sciences is important in development of theory, as is adherence to the best scientific methods available. "Thick and strong" concepts are preferred to "thin and weak" concepts, in spite of the fact that it is easier to test and argue for weak and thin concepts. Reality is complex and should be reflected in the best available manner. Thick concepts that include humans and value and justice will not make the lives of economists any easier. The ethical relevance of economics is, however, dependent on this richness. Feminist economic research pertaining to ethics seems to attract much attention, which is due to the fruitful hypotheses that are waiting to be explored. From a justice perspective, this rich complexity is something to be wished for, but also a solid theoretical challenge, to think about economic theory in new ways.

Concern for lived reality is another similarity between feminist economists and ethicists. It is important to see it like it is, to acknowledge those who are most disadvantaged. To listen to stories of oppression is one way that feminists have obtained knowledge about injustice. The holistic tendency is also clear in the willingness to accommodate research from other fields. The development of a feminist critical theory, for example, is helpful to put reality in focus. Critical theory places the justice concept in a broader arena that includes social, legal, political, and other realms that impinge on the economic.

The challenge from feminist scholars is heard in many places and is being taken increasingly seriously. One example is how the World Bank now puts much effort into gender studies and policies.[39] There is also a new awareness of the importance of including women in development economics. By acknowledging women as a distinct category, it is possible to discern how statistics work to include or exclude more than half of the human race. Women's inclusion is due to at least two things: women are demanding to be included in the decisions about how common resources are handled, and there is a growing knowledge about women's work in the informal and formal sector and in family planning. Those inclusions of women happen in policy-making bodies. But when it comes to the boardrooms of large companies, women are almost totally absent from the discussion.

Feminist economists have already started the transformative work of a more encompassing understanding of economics, which I am sure will influence further changes in economic theory and practice. But the road is difficult, and the resistance is hard. Women have a difficult time in economic research: there are not many positions open for those who do not conform to mainstream theory.[40]

A dignified way ahead lies in promoting the already-approved ideals of mutual respect and equality of all persons, expressed in everyone's option to obtain economic self-sufficiency. The way that feminist economists reconnect economics to ethics and morals is a new development in economic theory. Whether it will influence neoclassical economics remain to be seen.[41]

To achieve a feminist ethics for economics is no easy thing. Women differ vastly in their experiences, contexts, and ideological perspectives. I have chosen a relatively straightforward route by connecting directly to the poor when looking for a feminist theory of economic justice. An ethic of economics, whether feminist or not, that aims to improve the plight of the poor must include strong moral positions on equality, right relations, and liberation from oppression.

The fundamental requirement is that all able and willing persons should have the freedom to satisfy their own basic needs within existing economic systems. The assumption is that access to basic needs will increase liberation from oppression for women. The opportunity to satisfy one's basic needs is also significant for right relationships. Women who can support themselves may also organize and develop their capabilities to love and do justice.

NOTES

1. Market Economics and Feminist Economics

1. In 1993, the first feminist scholarly congress in economics took place in Amsterdam. "Out of the Margin" was the theme of the conference and of a resulting book. See Kuiper and Sap, *Out of the Margin,* and Humphries, *Gender and Economics.*

2. Lipsey et al., *Economics,* 3.

3. Ibid., 7, 220–323.

4. Smith, *Inquiry,* 157.

5. Lipsey et al., *Economics,* 329–32.

6. Ibid., 604–05, 610–11.

7. According to figures from UNCTAD presented in the newspaper *Dagens Nyheter,* in 1977 trade in goods amounted to $1.3 billion (U.S.), while trade in services and finance equaled $3.3 billion (U.S.). In 1990, the financial market encompassed $325 billion, and trade with goods had grown to only $4.8 billion. See *Dagens Nyheter,* A21.

8. Soros, "Can There Be a Global Economy?" George Soros delivered this paper in Stockholm; in it he critiqued the lack of regulations of the global financial market. He argued that this is a flaw in the non-market sector or governance of global society. Those with the task of making rules have no means of performing this task. Soros asks for universal values that he thinks are necessary to hold our global society together in its interaction with global capitalism.

9. World Bank, *World Development Indicators,* 3; UNDP, *Human Development Report,* 1998, 36.

10. UNDP, *Human Development Report,* 1998, 36.

11. UNDP, *Human Development Report,* 1995, 96–98. "Clearly the value of non-SNA[System of National Accounts] production in industrial countries is considerable, whatever the standard. It is at least half of GDP

[gross domestic product] and it accounts for more than half the private consumption."

12. Trafficking of women is a complex subject and involves many issues. For example, girls and women are often sent abroad by their families to be employed as house servants. This practice is encouraged by several countries in the Southern Hemisphere that are eager to obtain foreign currencies. Another form of trafficking sends women into forced prostitution under disastrous conditions. See Human Rights Watch, *Global Report on Women's Human Rights,* particularly the chapters on trafficking of women and girls and abuse against women workers. See also Rita Nakashima Brock and Susan Brooks Thistlethwaite, *Casting Stones: Prostitution and Liberation in Asia and the U.S.* (Minneapolis: Fortress Press, 1996).

13. Lipsey et al., 72–73.

14. Ibid., 220–21.

15. Ibid., 71–74.

16. Ibid., 167–70.

17. Ibid., 62.

18. Ibid., 60–74.

19. Smith, *Inquiry,* 191–92: "By preferring the support of domestic to that of foreign industry, he intends only his own security; and by directing that industry in such a manner as its produce may be of the greatest value, he intends only his own gain, and he is in this, as in many other cases led by an invisible hand to promote an end which was no part of his intention."

20. Lipsey et al., 105–25.

21. Ibid., 3–4, 18.

22. Ibid., 3.

23. The 1997 UNDP *Human Development Report* especially points out that it would not take a large portion of the available resources in the world to eliminate poverty in the world. To eradicate poverty would demand a mere 1 percent of the global income and 2 to 3 percent of the income in all but the very poorest countries. The resources to eradicate poverty in this generation are there, but they are not applied where needed. See UNDP, *Human Development Report,* 1997, 12.

24. Ibid., 113.

25. Ibid., 112–13.

26. Ibid., 12.

27. Ibid., 9, 107–10.

28. Lipsey et al., 26.

29. Ibid., 677.

30. Ibid., 187–92.

31. Ibid., 402–04.

32. Ibid., 27.

33. Ibid., 403. Two people stand out with their early warnings against environmental exploitation: Barbara Ward and E. F. Schumacher. See Ward, *Spaceship Earth;* and Schumacher, *Small Is Beautiful.*

34. See Boserup, *Women's Role in Economic Development.*

35. In a private consultation, Amartya Sen mentioned Esther Boserup as one of his early sources of inspiration.

36. In organizing the "Out of the Margin" conference in 1993, Edith Kuiper and Jolande Sap found that "the papers we received emerged from every perspective within economics: neoclassical, Marxian, post-Keynesian, institutional and Australian as well as more recent developments like social constructivism and postmodernism." Kuiper and Sap, *Out of the Margin,* 3.

37. Humphries, *Gender and Economics,* xiv.

38. Ferber and Nelson, *Beyond Economic Man,* 9–10.

39. Hartsock, *Money, Sex, and Power,* 117–18.

40. Nelson, *Feminism, Objectivity, and Economics,* xi, 132.

41. Ibid., 133.

42. Woolley, "Feminist Challenge," 4.

43. Ibid.

44. United Nations, *The World's Women,* 132–33. Data show that there are deviations from this heretofore accepted fact. In Australia, the United States, Denmark, and Sweden, women work less than men in paid and unpaid work taken together. The largest difference is the United States, where men work 59.5 hours a week while women work 56.4 hours a week. In Sweden the relationship is 60.5 hours for women and 61.2 hours for men; ibid., see also chart 5.2, 128, and 132–33. Also, here we can see the same exceptions regarding leisure time (see notes above).

45. Woolley, "Feminist Challenge," 5.

46. Nelson, *Feminism, Objectivity, and Economics,* 123–25.

47. Ibid., 42–43.

48. Waring, *If Women Counted.*

49. Harding, "Can Feminist Thought?" 7–33.

50. Ibid., 13–20.

51. Ibid., 14.

52. Ibid., 23–26. Harding denounces the value-neutral scientific ideal in favor of "standpoints" that include marginalized groups and their vantage points.

53. McCloskey, *Vices of Economists,* 15; Daly, *Gyn/ecology,* 39–40.

54. Nelson, *Feminism, Objectivity, and Economics,* 123. Nelson here refers to a critique of how economists deal with data.

55. Buruma, "Royal Comedy."

56. Jonásdottir, *Love, Power, and Political Interests,* 110–15.

57. Firestone, *Dialectic of Sex,* 139.

58. UNDP, *Human Development Report,* 1995, 96–98.

59. Hartmann, "Family as Locus," 374–75.

60. Ferber and Nelson, *Beyond Economic Man,* 5.

61. England, "Separative Self," 37–38.

62. Becker, "Altruism," 97–111.

63. Ibid., 98.

64. England, "Separative Self," 47–48.

65. Agarwal, "Bargaining and Gender Relations," 376–77.

66. Hartmann, "Family as Locus," 376–77.

67. Lipsey et al., *Economics,* 384.

68. Bergmann, *Economic Emergence,* 247.

69. Lipsey et al., *Economics,* 378.

70. Bergmann, *Economic Emergence,* 229.

71. Solow, "Feminist Theory," 156.

2. Feminist Critique of Objectivity and Empiricism in Economic Theory

1. Folbre, Who Pays? 20.

2. Ibid., 24–25.

3. Frank, Gilovich, and Regan, "Does Studying Economics Inhibit Cooperation?" 159–71. The conclusion of this study suggests that economists and students and professors of economists tend to act more in self-interested ways than non-economists and that men tend to have a significantly higher score on self-interest than women.

4. Lakoff and Johnson, *Metaphors;* Keller, *From a Broken Web.*

5. Nelson, *Feminism, Objectivity, and Economics,* 6–8.

6. Ferber and Nelson, *Beyond Economic Man,* 10.

7. Nelson, *Feminism, Objectivity, and Economics,* 7.

8. Ibid., 132–33.

9. Ibid., 142.

10. Ibid., 10.

11. Ibid.

12. Ibid., 26.

13. Ferber and Nelson, *Beyond Economic Man,* and Kuiper and Sap, *Out of the Margin,* are two anthologies with abundant arguments about the scientific aspects of economic science. Amartya Sen, in *On Ethics and Economics,* discusses the divide in economic theory between the more scientific/engineering economists and the ones who have a more ethics-oriented approach. His own ambition is to connect economics more closely to ethics and to the origin of economic theory, as it was taught together with moral philosophy at the time of Adam Smith.

14. Nelson, "Economic Theory and Feminist Theory," 120–24.

15. Humphries, *Gender and Economics*, xiv.

16. Nelson, *Feminism, Objectivity, and Economics*, 123–25.

17. Ibid., 128.

18. Folbre, *Who Pays for the Kids?* 47–50, 248.

19. Ibid., 49.

20. See Daly and Cobb, *For the Common Good*; George and Sabelli, *Faith and Credit*; Hartsock, *Money, Sex, and Power*; and Robertson, *Future Wealth*.

21. This critique was highlighted by Marilyn Waring in *If Women Counted*.

22. Ibid., 33–35; Ferber and Nelson, *Beyond Economic Man*, 5.

23. Waring, *If Women Counted*, 15–16.

24. United Nations, *World's Women* 1995, 107.

25. Bergmann, *Economic Emergence*, 120–23.

26. Ibid., 9–10.

27. Ibid., 125–26.

28. Ibid., 121, table 6.1.

29. United Nations, *The World's Women*, 128, chart 5.20.

30. Nelson, Feminism, *Objectivity, and Economics*, 55.

31. Buchanan, *What Should Economists Do?* Buchanan argues with Gunnar Myrdal's critique of the presumed objectivity of social sciences and says that if Myrdal is right, then there is no truth to economic theory at all (136). Buchanan positions himself where normative discourse is placed outside of economic science.

32. Galtung, *Theory and Method*, 28.

33. "Validitet," in *Nationalencyklopedin*, vol. 19, 204.

34. See Galtung, *Theory and Method*, 27–29, and Föllestad, Walö, and Elster, *Argumentasjonsteroi*, 73.

35. Bergström, *Objektivitet*.

36. Ibid., 67–78, 70.

37. Ibid., 121–22.

38. Harding, "Can Feminist Thought?" 18.

39. Ibid., 14.

40. Kuhn, *Structure of Scientific Revolution*.

41. Harding, "Can Feminist Thought?" 24.

42. Bergström, *Objektivitet*, 98–103.

43. Nelson, *Feminism, Objectivity, and Economics*, 51–56.

44. Folbre, *Who Pays?* 18.

45. Nelson, *Feminism, Objectivity, and Economics*, 41.

46. Ibid., 42.

47. Ibid., 45.

48. Ibid., 46.

49. Bergström, *Objektivitet*, 56–60.

50. Nelson, *Feminism, Objectivity, and Economics*, 44.

51. Folbre, *Who Pays?* 20.

52. Ibid., 55–56.

53. Nelson, *Feminism, Objectivity, and Economics*, 31–33.

54. Ibid., 69.

55. Folbre, *Who Pays?* 25. James Stuart Mill, father of John Stuart Mill, in 1825 formulated "joint utility" as a concept to denounce the need for a separate women's franchise. Women's interests were taken care of by their husbands and fathers. Gary Becker is the most well known contemporary economist who theorizes out of the "joint utility" concept, which he has expanded.

56. Nelson, *Feminism, Objectivity, and Economics*, 62.

57. Ibid., 63.

58. Folbre, *Who Pays?* 40–43.

59. Ibid., 54.

60. Ibid., 60.

61. Ibid., 4.

62. Ibid., 223.

63. Gita Sen and Grown, *Development Crises*, 43–44.

64. Nelson, *Feminism, Objectivity, and Economics*, 36.

65. Ibid., 118.

66. Nelson, "The Study of Choice," 33.

67. See Humphries, *Gender and Economics;* Kuiper and Sap, *Out of the Margin;* and Folbre, *Economics of the Family.*

68. Folbre, *Who Pays?* 249.

69. Ibid., 252.

3. Equality, Rights, Power, and Basic Human Needs in Feminist Development Economics

1. Gita Sen is one of the founding members of Development Alternatives for Women in a New Era (DAWN). Together with Caren Grown, she wrote *Development Crises and Alternative Visions: Third World Women's Perspectives.*

2. South Asia refers here to Pakistan, Bangladesh, India, and Sri Lanka.

3. Agarwal, *Field of One's Own*, 2.

4. Ibid., 38.

5. Ibid., 449.

6. Gita Sen and Grown, *Development Crises.* Their organization, DAWN, was founded in Bangalore, India, in 1982. Presently it has its head-

quarters in Barbados. The authors give credit for the development of the book to the many women involved in the process, which was initiated as a part of the UN's decade for women, 1975–85. Gita is a professor of economics in Bangalore and an adjunct professor at the Harvard's Center for Population and Development Studies.

7. Gita Sen and Grown, *Development Crises,* 18–19.

8. Ibid., 23.

9. Ibid., 24. As mentioned before, the unaccounted work of women was until recently neglected in the system of national accounts. The change in the account system is presented in chapter 7.

10. Ibid., 28.

11. Ibid., 20.

12. Ibid., 40.

13. Ibid., 43.

14. Ibid., 39.

15. Agarwal, *Field of One's Own,* 19–20.

16. Agarwal, "Gender, Property, and Land Rights," 246–47.

17. The legal system in India is complicated in matters of civil justice. Agarwal gives an extensive account of how the legal systems in India function for Hindus, Muslims, and Christians.

18. Agarwal, "Gender, Property, and Land Rights," 270–71.

19. Ibid., 281–82.

20. Ibid., 278.

21. Ibid., 280–81.

22. Ibid., 28–29. This particular statistic refers to research done in many states in India about how men and women in poor households spend their money.

23. Agarwal, *Field of One's Own,* 27–33.

24. Ibid., 35.

25. Grameen Bank was founded by Professor Muhammed Yunus at the University of Dacca in 1983.The policy to provide poor women with microloans began in 1985. Microloans are small loans that are given directly to people who most likely have had no previous contact with banks and are not able to get regular loans because they are regarded as bad risks. Microloaning is now a whole movement directed to poor women and collectives. It has been a very successful banking activity that is now also sponsored by the World Bank (see Khandker, Khalily, and Khan, *Grameen Bank Performance and Sustainability*). Ninety-four percent of the borrowers are women and the repayment rate of loans is 90 percent. By 1994, Grameen Bank served half of the villages in Bangladesh with a total membership of over 2 million. The bank has received serious attention from international institutions and has been a major inspiration in the

development of microloans. Khandker, Khalily, and Khan write: "The Grameen Bank experience suggests that it is possible to develop a profitable financial institution that exclusively works with the poor" (xiii).

26. Agarwal, *Field of One's Own*, 36.

27. Ibid., 51–52. The relationship between genders is both cooperative and conflicting. The power relations between men and women are manifest in a wide variety of areas, among them class, caste, and race. They are socially constructed and vary over time. Relations between genders may also change through bargaining over time. Women contest gender hierarchy in three ways: (1) in *form*—that is, individually or in groups; (2) in *content*—that is, in economics, social, or political rules, practices, and institutions; and (3) in different *arenas*—the family, the market, the state.

28. Gita Sen and Grown, *Development Crises*, 49.

29. Daly and Cobb, *For the Common Good*, 35–43. The "fallacy of misplaced concreteness" originated with process theologian Alfred Whitehead as a critique of a tendency within science to distance itself more and more from reality and instead construct abstract models from which scientists then make far-reaching predictions about reality.

30. Bunch and Fisher, *What Future?*

31. Hartsock, *Money, Sex, and Power*, 225–26.

32. Agarwal, "Gender, Property, and Land Rights," 276.

33. Ibid., 284.

34. Ibid., 277.

35. Agarwal, *Field of One's Own*, 39.

36. Agarwal, "Bargaining and Gender Relations."

37. Ibid., 3–4. Formal discussions about household economics started with the work of Gary Becker.

38. Agarwal, "Bargaining and Gender Relations," 2.

39. Ibid., 7–8.

40. Ibid., 20–21.

41. Ibid., 21.

42. Gita Sen, "Poverty, Economic Growth, and Gender Equity," 31.

43. Gita Sen and Grown, *Development Crises*, 67–74.

44. The first Special Session on Disarmament was held in 1978. The second Special Session on Disarmament was held in 1982 in New York, and the peace march in connection with this session was reported to have rallied one million people. The third conference was held in 1988, also in New York.

45. Gita Sen and Grown, *Development Crises*, 89.

46. Gita Sen, "Poverty, Economic Growth, and Gender Equity," 50.

47. Gita Sen and Grown, *Development Crises*, 17. The critique that is put forth by many development economists is aimed at the Structural

Adjustment Programs (SAPs) that the World Bank enforces as a condition for loans and assistance to countries that are afflicted by economic difficulties. See Susan George's *The Debt Boomerang*.

48. Gita Sen and Grown, *Development Crises*, 38.

49. World Bank, *World Bank Research Program*, 17.

50. Lynn Bennett, *Women, Poverty, and Productivity in India*, 51.

51. Gita Sen and Grown, *Development Crises*, 43–44.

52. The demand to put a value on women's work in the informal sector has been strongly emphasized in feminist theory and agreed upon by the UN only as recently as the 1990s. For more on this discussion, see chapter 7.

53. Gita Sen and Grown, *Development Crises*, 18, 23; Gita Sen, "Reproduction," 5.

54. Agarwal, "Gender, Property, and Land Rights," 268.

55. Amartya Sen, *Resources, Values, and Development*. Amartya Sen here explores faulty distribution of food and lack of democracy as factors that increase famines.

56. Weston, Falk, and D'Amato, *Basic Documents*.

4. Liberation Theology and Feminism

1. Mary Daly, who started out as a theologian, is an icon in both feminist theory and feminist philosophy, and her influence has been tremendous.

2. In fact, most feminist theologians would claim some influence from liberation theology.

3. Schubeck, *Liberation Ethics*, 22. Praxis is a central concept in Marxist theory, where it means reflection on the epistemological process that relates theory and theory-informed practice. See *Nationalencyklopedin*, vol. 15, 259. The use of praxis in most liberation theology adheres to Marxist theory and method.

4. See King, *Feminist Theology*.

5. Cannon, "Hitting," 33–39.

6. Schubeck, *Liberation Ethics*, 46–47. Here Schubeck traces the influence of Paulo Freire on Latin American liberation theology. He also traces the influences of G. W. F. Hegel and Karl Marx on Freire's understanding of praxis. In Freire's version, praxis is included in conscientization and has more spiritual connotations (from Hegel) than Marxist praxis has.

7. Freire, *Pedagogy*, 20, 27–33.

8. *Practice* is a reference to a nonreflective usage that is different from the word *praxis*.

9. Freire, *Pedagogy*, 33.

10. Gutiérrez, *Theology of Liberation*, 91–92. Gutiérrez was among liberation theology's founders and gave this theology its name.

11. Ibid., 89.

12. Ibid., 26–27.

13. Ibid., 91.

14. Ibid., 32.

15. A description of Christian realism will come in the next chapter.

16. Bennett, *Radical Imperative*, 131–41.

17. Schubeck, *Liberation Ethics*, 222–25. Here Schubeck reviews the arguments for an armed revolution that are put forth by José Míguez Bonino.

18. See the essays by Julia Esquivel and Elsa Tamez in Eck and Jain, *Speaking of Faith*, 19, 29, 30–38. This book is a report from a conference organized by Harvard University on women, religion, and social change.

19. Grenholm, *Christian Social Ethics*, 222–26.

20. Alison Jaggar's book *Feminist Politics and Human Nature* gives a good presentation of the differences between liberal, radical, and socialist feminisms.

21. Ibid., 353.

22. Gutiérrez, *Theology of Liberation*, 15. "It is for all these reasons that the theology of liberation offers us not so much a new theme for reflection as *a new way* to do theology. Theology as critical reflection on historical praxis is a liberating theology, a theology of the liberating transformation of the history of mankind and also therefore that part of mankind—gathered here into *ecclesia*—which openly confesses Christ."

23. Ibid., 107.

24. Schubeck, *Liberation Ethics*, 221.

25. Feinberg, *Social Philosophy*, 65–66.

26. Schubeck, *Liberation Ethics*, 63.

27. Ibid., 65.

28. Ibid., 64–65.

29. Ibid., 67.

30. Gutiérrez, *Theology of Liberation*, 13, 24, 39–49.

31. Fiorenza, *In Memory of Her*, 26–36.

32. Stanton, *Eighty Years*, 389–92.

33. Fiorenza, *In Memory of Her*, 7–14. Fiorenza views Stanton as standing in the feminist tradition of hermeneutics. Stanton's understanding of how the Bible was handled at that time and interpreted by men was an early example of how women have long struggled with the Bible. Their intuition and their arguments are still valid, and Stanton's arguments put her in the tradition of historical critical exegesis.

34. Ibid., 34.

35. Schubeck, *Liberation Ethics*, 84.

36. Arendt, *Human Condition*, 200.

37. Bóasdóttir, *Violence*.

38. Schubeck, *Liberation Ethics*, 11, 151.

39. Hunt, *Feminist Liberation Theology*, 147–51.

40. The literature is vast, but a good overview can be obtained in Kittay and Meyers, *Women and Moral Theory*.

41. Freire, *Pedagogy*, 33. Humanization is a goal for human conduct in the writing of Paulo Freire. In this short quotation we are confronted with many of the difficulties between feminism and Latin American machismo.

42. Iris Young, *Justice*, 13.

5. Feminist Ethics and Economics

1. Harrison, *Making Connections*, 55.

2. Bennett, *Radical Imperative*, 156.

3. Liberal theology is recognized for its emphasis on the ethical dimensions of religious life. At its inception, the simple teachings of Jesus were at the center of attention, and the theological arena was reduced. Personal justification, salvation, a good life, and the normative aspects of the teachings of Jesus were emphasized, while the transcendent aspects in theology and Christology were neglected or denied. The leading motivations were enlightenment, science, and knowledge. The most well known liberal theologians were Albrecht Ritschl, Wilhelm Herrmann, and Adolf von Harnack.

4. Troeltsch, *Social Teaching*. Troeltsch gives a thorough review of how there have always been movements that want to make a radical break from society to live in greater harmony with the biblical imperatives about the good Christian life, according to their own understanding. Troeltsch pays particular interest to how the Sermon on the Mount has been used in such revival movements.

5. Harrison, *Our Right to Choose*, 76–78.

6. Secord and Backman, *Social Psychology*, 115–19. Festinger's theory about cognitive dissonance was introduced already in 1957 (if you don't think Paul did so), and he gives an account of why people who know that something is right still do the wrong thing. For instance, the dangers of smoking are well known to smokers, but they will often continue to smoke.

7. Niebuhr, *Christian Realism*, 106.

8. Ibid., 106–07, 117–45. Niebuhr's premises, that we must adhere to political realism in a Machiavellian sense, are presented in an article about Augustine, whom Niebuhr praises as the theologian most well versed in matters of self-knowledge regarding human nature. Opposing the force of

Christian love is the human inclination to self-love and self-interest, the not-so-virtuous traits of human nature.

9. Lebacqz, *Six Theories*, 84–85.

10. Ibid., 98.

11. Harrison, *Making the Connections*, 58–59.

12. Lebacqz, *Six Theories*, 87.

13. Harrison, *Making the Connections*, 59, 67.

14. Lebacqz, *Six Theories*, 89.

15. Niebuhr, *Christian Realism*, 33–43. The chapter "Why Is Communism So Evil?" 1953, provides a presentation of Niebuhr's stance on communism and Marxism. He opposes the monopoly of power by the working class, which will inevitably produce injustice (34). The power position of the communist party is supported by "the whole series of pretensions derived from the secular religion which creates the ethos of the Communist Society. . . . The utopian illusions presumably make communism more dangerous rather than more evil." He maintains that its utopian illusions make communism more dangerous than Nazism. The reason for this is that the utopian visions have the capacity to convince people of the inherently good purpose of communism (36–37).

16. Harrison, *Making the Connections*, 60.

17. Ibid., 61–62.

18. Ibid.

19. Ibid., 63.

20. Niebuhr, *Christian Realism*, 50–51; Harrison, *Making Connections*, 58, 63.

21. Harrison, *Making the Connections*, 65.

22. Ibid., 65.

23. Ibid., 59.

24. Ibid., 55–56, 68.

25. Ibid., 70.

26. Niebuhr, *Moral Man*, 21–22.

27. Ibid., 57.

28. Lebacqz, *Six Theories*, 86.

29. Niebuhr, *Moral Man*, 80.

30. Harrison, *Making the Connections*, 15–16.

31. Ibid., 55–57.

32. Ibid., 56–57.

33. Jaggar, *Feminist Politics*, 125–32.

34. See Benhabib et al., *Feminist Contentions;* and Meehan, *Feminists Read Habermas.*

35. Fraser, "False Antithesis," 59–60. The critical issue has been in part to clarify the distinction between poststructuralism and critical theory and

determine if one or the other is compatible with feminist theory. The work of philosopher Nancy Fraser has delved into these questions, and she maintains that poststructural theory is disguised in postmodern theory and that this blurs the issue. Furthermore, she is in disagreement that the two approaches are indeed irreconcilable. Ibid.

36. Fraser, "What's Critical?" 21.
37. Fraser, *Justice Interruptus,* 19.
38. Ibid., 12.
39. Ibid., 13–15.
40. Ibid., 12.
41. Harrison, *Making the Connections,* 55.
42. Ibid., 69–70.
43. Ibid., 56.
44. Ibid., 70–71.
45. Ibid., 72.
46. Ibid., 73.
47. Ibid., 73–74.
48. Ibid., 75.
49. Ibid., 76.
50. Ibid., 77.
51. Ibid., 255.
52. Ibid., 253.
53. Ibid., 253–55.
54. Ibid., 18.
55. Here Harrison is indebted to the work of Dorothee Soelle.
56. Harrison, *Making the Connections,* 15–16.
57. Ibid., 232.
58. Ibid., 231.
59. See, for example, Anette Baier, "Hume," 175–77. She particularly emphasizes how Hume abandons the idea of an inherent structure of the subject and says that what we can observe is a bundle of feelings.
60. Ibid.
61. Benhabib, *Situating the Self,* 29.
62. Harrison, *Making the Connections,* 80.
63. Ibid., 251.

6. A Feminist Approach to Justice

1. Lebacqz, *Six Theories*, 50.
2. Ibid., 64–65.
3. Ibid., 121.
4. Ibid., 52.
5. Ibid., 56–57.
6. Lebacqz, *Justice*, 53.
7. Lebacqz, *Six Theories*, 120.
8. Ibid., 121.
9. Benhabib, *Situating the Self*.
10. Ibid., 16.
11. Ibid., 155.
12. Ibid., 29.
13. Benhabib, "Feminism and Postmodernism," 48–51. In this essay, Benhabib gives an interesting review of what can be salvaged by feminism from the all-encompassing concepts of Western history and culture.
14. Lebacqz, *Justice*, 11, 150.
15. Ibid., 72.
16. Ibid., 62–66.
17. Ibid., 59.
18. Ibid., 70.
19. Morton, *Journey Is Home*, 178–202. Here Nelle Morton tells an important story about a cognitive moment in the women's movement. Part of the story includes a meeting at the Seminary Quarter at Grailville, Ohio, in 1976, which I attended. She stressed the importance of listening so that women would talk. Her description of how women changed in the course of telling their stories is a classic in feminist theology, and she is quoted widely for this, including by Harrison, Christine Keller, Lebacqz, Mary Daly, and Marilyn Frye.
20. Lebacqz, *Justice*, 14.
21. Trible, *Texts of Terror*.
22. Lebacqz, *Six Theories*, 101.
23. Ibid., 112.
24. Iris Young, *Justice*, 48–53.
25. Lebacqz, *Justice*, 27–30.
26. Iris Young, *Justice*, 56–58.
27. Lebacqz, *Justice*, 61–62.
28. Iris Young, *Justice*, 58–61.
29. Lebacqz, *Justice*, 24–27.
30. Ibid., 77.
31. Lebacqz, *Six Theories*, 108.
32. Lebacqz, *Justice*, 64.

33. Pamela Young, *Feminist Theology/Christian Theology,* 49–56.

34. Schleiermacher, "General Hermeneutics," 73.

35. Lebacqz, *Justice,* 155.

36. Harrison, *Making Connections,* 255.

7. Basic Human Needs: A Criterion for Justice

1. Harrison, *Making Connections,* 255.

2. Lebacqz, *Six Theories,* 107.

3. UNDP, *Human Development Report,* 1996, 32.

4. Fraser, *Unruly Practices.* See chapters 7 and 8.

5. Universal Human Rights Declaration, 1948, article 25: "(1) Everyone has the right to a standard of living adequate for the health and well-being of himself and of his family, including food, clothing, housing and medical care and necessary social services, and the right to security in the event of unemployment, sickness, disability, widowhood, old age or other lack of livelihood in circumstances beyond his control. (2) Motherhood and childhood are entitled to special care and assistance. All children, whether born in or out of wedlock, shall enjoy the same social protection." In Weston, Falk, and D'Amato, *Basic Documents,* 300.

6. Drèze and Amartya Sen, *Hunger and Public Action.* See chapter 3 on Nutrition and Capability.

7. Maslow, *Psychology of Being,* 22.

8. UNDP, *Human Development Report,* 1996, 38–42.

9. It cannot be stressed enough that the "right-to-life" language here comes out of global policy publications. It refers to persons' right to such resources as will enable them to continue living. The right-to -ife language shall be interpreted in connection with United Nations protocols, conventions, laws, and declarations. It should not be confused with the antiabortion movement in the United States.

10. UNDP, *Human Development Report,* 1996, 56.

11. Mies and Shiva, *Ecofeminism,* 79–82.

12. Daly and Cobb, *For the Common Good,* 135.

13. Maslow, *Psychology of Being,* 220.

14. Lutz and Lux, *Humanistic Economics,* 9, 12–13. When Lutz and Lux look at Maslow's needs hierarchy, they use his idea of self-actualization as the ultimate achievement.

15. Fraser, *Unruly Practices,* 183.

16. Lipsey, et al., *Economics.* "Economics is the study of the use of scarce resources to satisfy unlimited human wants" (3).

17. UNDP, *Human Development Report ,*1996, 47–50.

18. International Labor Organization, *Employment*, 3. Poverty in these statistics refers to people who survive on less than a dollar a day.

19. Bryant, "Conditions," 230.

20. Ibid., 236.

21. UNDP, *Human Development Report*, 1997, discusses a Human Poverty Index (HPI), developed to describe what happens at the bottom of development and social community. A comprehensive review of "social underdevelopment" is presented by Ruth Leger Sivard in *World Military and Social Expenditures*, 26–29.

22. Nelson, *Feminism, Objectivity, and Economics*, 34.

23. Collste, *Makten*, 51–62.

24. Ibid., 54.

25. Ibid., 225.

26. Maslow, *Psychology of Being*, 199–200.

27. Lutz and Lux, *Humanist Economics*, 9–11.

28. UNDP, *Human Development Report*, 1996, 47–54.

29. O´Neill, "Justice," 312.

30. The four international conferences that the United Nations have conducted on women have all had the same title: *Equality, Development and Peace*.

31. Agarwal, *Field of One's Own*, 34–35.

32. Ibid., 4.

33. Drèze and Amartya Sen, *Hunger and Public Action*, 12–13.

34. Amartya Sen, "Capability," 30–31.

35. Liss, *Health Care Needs*, 63–64.

36. Ibid., 45–65.

37. "Everyone has the right to life, liberty and the security of person," article 3 in the Universal Declaration of Human Rights (1948); "Everyone's right to life shall be protected by law," in article 2 of the European Convention for the protection of human rights and fundamental freedoms (1950). "Every human being has the inherent right to life. This right shall be protected by law. No one shall be arbitrarily deprived of his life," article 6 in International Covenant on Civil and Political Rights. "Every person has the right to have his life respected, " article 4 in American Convention on Human Rights (1969). "Every human being shall be entitled to respect for his life and the integrity of his person," article 4 in African Charter on Human and People's Rights (1981). Weston, Falk, and D'Amato, *Basic Documents*, 298, 302, 377, 398, 449.

38. Harrison, *Making Connections*, 8.

39. Lebacqz, *Justice*, 159.

40. Ibid., 11.

41. Held, "Feminism and Moral Theory," 112–15.

42. Held, "Meshing," 131.
43. Benhabib, *Situating the Self,* 200–01.
44. Waring, *If Women Counted,* 49.
45. Daly and Cobb, *For the Common Good,* 83.
46. Ibid., 62–76.
47. Lipsey, et al., *Economics,* 486.
48. Ibid., 488–499.
49. United Nations, *The World's Women,* 107.
50. Moon, *Political Economy.*
51. Morris, *Measuring,* 8–14; Moon, *Political Economy,* 3–4, 20–22.
52. Morris, *Measuring,* 82–87.
53. Moon, *Political Economy,* 25–26.
54. Streeten et al., *First Things First,* 88–89.
55. Daly and Cobb, *For the Common Good,* 371–73.
56. UNDP, *Human Development Report,* 1996, 28–31, 106.
57. Ibid., box 1.6, 34, 107–8.
58. Ibid., 27–28, 109–10.
59. Ibid., 154.
60. Ibid., 159.
61. United Nations, *The World's Women,* 129.
62. Kymlika, *Contemporary Political Philosophy,* 239.
63. World Bank, *Toward Gender Equality,* 14.
64. United Nations, *The World's Women,* 70.
65. Ibid., 66–67.
66. At the UN World Summit on Social Development in Copenhagen, March 1995, a tribunal on crimes against women was conducted. Women gave testimonies about hideous injustices that they had endured. A woman from India told the story of how she had been forced to murder four of her own female children before she escaped the marriage and its relations. See also Amartya Sen, "Women's Survival."

8. A Feminist Theory of Economic Justice

1. Goldberg and Kremen, *Feminization of Poverty;* Robb and Casebolt, *Covenant;* Robb, *Equal Value;* Bounds, Brubaker, and Hobgood, *Welfare Policy.*
2. Nelson, *Feminism, Objectivity, and Economics,* 34–35, 124–25.
3. Folbre, *Who Pays?* 18–25, 54.
4. Lebacqz, *Justice,* 150–54.
5. Harrison, *Making Connections,* 75–77.
6. Ibid., 253–55.

7. Amartya Sen, "Capability." This article gives a comprehensive presentation of the capability concept, which Sen applies to his welfare thinking. He was granted the Nobel Prize in Economics in 1998.

8. Ibid., 31.

9. UNDP, *Human Development Report,* 1996, 109–10. As presented in chapter 7, the Capability Poverty Measure includes (1) number of births attended by trained personnel, (2) compared weight of children under five, and (3) women's illiteracy rate.

10. UNDP, *Human Development Report,* 1997, box 6.4, 112.

11. UNDP, *Human Development Report,* 1996, 201. Here the world comparison is between 1985, when it amounted to $792 billion, compared to 1994's $778 billion, while the percentage of GDP was 4.3 in 1985 and 3.2 in 1994. So, percentage-wise the amount is lower, but in actual dollars it is the same. The World Bank (*World Bank Development Indicators,* 1998, 278–81) makes a similar comparison: in 1985 it estimated the GNP percentage to be 5.2, and in 1995, 2.8. The World Bank abstains from giving any amounts in actual dollars. The figures measure somewhat different things and refer to different measures of national productions. The UN's revised System of National Accounts from 1993 is not followed.

12. Harrison, *Making Connections,* 18.

13. Ibid., 19.

14. Lebacqz, *Justice,* 158–59. When discussing Christian love, Harrison is especially critical of the theme of sacrificial love prevalent in Christian theology.

15. Sandra Harding, Cathrine Keller.

16. Michael Walzer, Amatai Etzioni, Martha Nussbaum.

17. This formula was firmly set down at the UN Human Rights Conference in Vienna in 1994. See Bunch and Reilly, *Demanding Accountability.*

18. Every time the UN discusses a change in any charter, declaration, convention, or protocol, it confronts a very difficult situation and conflicting interests. The relatively coherent and dominant Western culture that gave birth to many of those documents is no longer at hand. It should be noted that this does not necessarily involve a North–South split. At the UN's Fourth Conference on Women in Beijing in 1995, the most radical language regarding oppression came from South Africa, whose new constitution is the most radical in the world in its language against all forms of oppression against people for any reason. At the same time, the Vatican did its utmost to limit women's access to contraceptives and abortion.

19. Amartya Sen, *Inequality Reexamined,* 19–20.

20. The UN Universal Declaration of Human Rights is a focal point when it comes to a universal understanding of rights and equality. Looking

at it more than fifty years after its inception, it remains a very modern document still in search of implementation.

21. Amartya Sen, *Inequality Reexamined*, 12–30.

22. Ibid., 13–14.

23. For a thorough treatment of the issue of equal value according to Christian theology, see Grenholm, *Protestant Work Ethics*, 259, 261, 268.

24. Bóasdóttir, *Violence, Power, and Justice*, 187. Bóasdóttir critiques Christian theological tradition on many accounts for its assumptions about ontological differences between men and women. She rejects ontological differences between the sexes, as do I and most other feminist ethicists.

25. Weston, Falk, and D'Amato, *Basic Documents*, 443–47.

26. UNDP, *Human Development Report*, 1996, 109–10.

27. Amartya Sen, *Inequality Reexamined*, 30.

28. As is shown by the Gender Empowerment Measure (GEM), composed by UNDP.

29. Pujol, "Into the Margin!"

30. UNDP, *Human Development Report*, 1997, 154.

31. There are still situations in which women are legally forbidden access to the labor market; Afghanistan until recently was an example of this. Pressure from the global community to erase this kind of inequality is considerable.

32. Barbara Bergmann is a vocal defendant of affirmative action as well as a socialist-feminist economist. She analyzes marginal productivity and the arguments that the market will set the right wage irrespective of gender and sex in her essay "Occupational Segregation Wages and Profits When Employers Discriminate by Race or Sex," 1974, 103–10, reprinted 1995 in *Gender and Economics*, ed. Jane Humphries.

33. Iris Young, *Justice*, 33–36.

34. Sivard, *World Military and Social Expenditures*, 30.

35. The UN System of National Accounts (UNSNA) is continually pressured to fill in the information gap about the informal sector. The latest resolution, though not the first, to include the informal sector in economic accounts comes from the UN's Fourth International Women's Conference in Beijing, 1995. What has been done until now suggests that the informal sector is at least as important as the traditional GDP measure.

36. Harrison, *Making Connections*, 68–69.

37. Ibid., 80.

38. Folbre, *Who Pays?* 27–29.

39. The International Bank for Reconstruction and Development (IBRD), commonly known as the World Bank, is active in many fields and also has an extensive research department. However, this department is not in charge of what the bank does when it functions as a bank.

40. Ferber and Nelson, *Beyond Economic Man,* 2–4.

41. The issue of ethics in economics has been pinpointed by Amartya Sen in *On Ethics and Economics.*

BIBLIOGRAPHY

Agarwal, Bina. "Bargaining and Gender Relations: Within and beyond the Household." *Feminist Economics* 3, no. 1 (spring 1997): 1–50.

———. *A Field of One's Own: Gender and Land Rights in South Asia.* Vol. 58 of *Cambridge South Asian Studies.* Cambridge: Cambridge Univ. Press, 1994.

———. "Gender and Command over Property: A Critical Gap in Economic Analysis and Policy in South Asia." *World Development* 22, no. 10 (1994): 1455–78.

———. "Gender, Property, and Land Rights: Bridging a Gap in Economic Analysis and Policy." In *Out of the Margin: Feminist Perspectives on Economics,* edited by Edith Kuiper and Jolande Sap. London: Routledge, 1995.

Althaus, Paul. *The Ethics of Martin Luther.* Philadelphia: Fortress Press, 1972.

Anderson, Elizabeth. *Value in Ethics and Economics.* Cambridge: Harvard Univ. Press, 1993.

Arendt, Hannah. *The Human Condition.* 1958. Reprint, Chicago: Univ. of Chicago Press, 1989.

Aslaneigui, Nahid, Steven Pressman, and Gale Summerfield, eds. *Women in the Age of Economic Transformation: Gender Impact of Reforms in Postsocialist and Developing Countries.* London: Routledge, 1994.

Atherton, John. *Christianity and the Market: Christian Social Thought for Our Time.* London: SPCK, 1992.

Baier, Anette. "Hume: The Women's Moral Theorist." In *Women and Moral Theory,* edited by Eva Feder Kittay and Diana T. Meyers. Totowa, N.J.: Rowman & Littlefield, 1987.

Bakker, Isabella, ed. *The Strategic Silence: Gender and Economic Policy.* London: Zed Books, 1994.

Barten, Anton P. "Family Composition, Prices and Expenditure Patterns." In *Econometric Analysis for National Economic Planning,* edited by P. E. Hart, G. Mills, and J. K.Whittaker. London: Butterworth, 1964.

Beauvoir, Simone de. *The Second Sex.* 1949. Reprint, Hamondsworth, England: Penguin Books, 1972.

Becker, Gary S. "Altruism in the Family and Selfishness in the Market Place." In *The Economics of the Family,* edited by Nancy Folbre. Cheltenham, England: Edward Elgar Publishing, 1996.

Benhabib, Seyla. "Feminism and Postmodernism: An Uneasy Alliance." In *Feminist Contentions,* edited by Seyla Benhabib, Judith Butler, Drucilla Cornell, and Nancy Fraser, New York: Routledge, 1995.

―――. *Situating the Self: Gender, Community, and Postmodernism in Contemporary Ethics.* New York: Routledge, 1992.

Benhabib, Seyla, and Drucilla Cornell, eds. *Feminism as Critique: Essays on the Politics of Gender in Late-Capitalist Societies.* Cambridge, England: Polity Press, 1987.

Benhabib, Seyla, and Fred Dallalmayr, eds. *The Communicative Ethics Controversy.* Cambridge: MIT Press, 1990.

Benhabib, Seyla, Judith Butler, Drucilla Cornell, and Nancy Fraser, eds. *Feminist Contentions: A Philosophical Exchange.* New York: Routledge, 1995.

Bennett, John C. *The Radical Imperative.* Philadelphia: Westminster Press, 1975.

Bennett, Lynn. *Women, Poverty, and Productivity in India.* EDI Seminar Paper, no. 43. Washington D.C.: Economic Development Institute of the World Bank, 1991.

Bergmann, Barbara R. *The Economic Emergence of Women.* New York: Basic Books, 1986.

―――. "Occupational Segregation Wages and Profits When Employers Discriminate by Race or Sex." *Eastern Economic Journal* 1, no. 2/3 (1974): 103–10.

Bergström, Lars. *Objektivitet.* Stockholm: Bokförlaget Thales, 1972.

Björkhem, Barbro, ed. *Samhällsguiden.* Stockholm: Fritzes, 1996.

Bóasdóttir, Sólveig Anna. *Violence, Power, and Justice: A Feminist Contribution to Christian Sexual Ethics.* Uppsala: Acta Universitatis Upsaliensis, 1998.

Boserup, Esther. *Women's Role in Economic Development.* New York: St. Martin's Press, 1970.

Boserup, Esther, and Christina Liljekrantz. *Integration and Women in Development: Why, When, How.* New York: UNDP, 1975.

Boulding, Elise. *Women in the Twentieth Century World.* New York: Halstead Press, 1977.

Boulding, Kenneth E. *The Meaning of the Twentieth Century.* San Francisco: Harper & Row, 1964.

Bounds, Elizabeth M. *Coming Together/Coming Apart: Religion, Community, and Modernity.* New York: Routledge, 1997.

Bounds, Elizabeth M., Pamela K. Brubaker, and Mary E. Hobgood, eds. *Welfare Policy: Feminist Critiques.* Cleveland: Pilgrim Press, 1999.

Brubaker, Pamela K. *Women Don't Count: The Challenge of Women's Poverty to Christian Ethics.* American Academy of Religion, no. 87. Atlanta: Scholars Press, 1994.

Bryant, William D. A. "Conditions for the Existence of Market Equilibrium." *Journal of Economic Education* 28, no. 3 (1977): 230–54.

Buchanan, James M. *What Should Economists Do?* Indianapolis: Liberty Press, 1979.

————. "A Broom of One's Own: Notes on the Women's Liberation Program." In *An Anthology of Women's Liberation by The New Women,* edited by Joanne Coole, Charlotte Bunch-Weeks, and Robin Morgan. Greenwich, Conn.: Fawcett World Library, 1971.

Bunch, Charlotte. *Passionate Politics: Feminist Theory in Action.* New York: St. Martin's Press, 1987.

Bunch, Charlotte, and Beverly Fisher. "What Future for Leadership." *Quest a Feminist Quarterly* 2, no. 4 (1976): 213.

Bunch, Charlotte, and Niamh Reilly. *Demanding Accountability: The Global Campaign and Vienna Tribunal for Women's Human Rights.* New York: Center for Women's Global Leadership and UNIFEM, 1994.

Buruma, Ian. "Royal Comedy." *New York Review of Books,* vol. 44, no. 15 (1997).

Buvinic, Mayra, Margaret A. Lycette, and William Paul McGreevey, eds. *Women and Poverty in the Third World.* Baltimore: Johns Hopkins Univ. Press, 1983.

Cannon, Katie G. "Hitting a Straight Lick with a Crooked Stick: The Womanist Dilemma in the Development of a Black Liberation Ethic." In *Feminist Theological Ethics,* edited by Lois K. Daly. Louisville: Westminster John Knox Press, 1994. 33–39.

Coletta, Nat J., Markus Kostner, and Ingo Wiederhofer. *The Transition from War to Peace in Sub-Saharan Africa.* Washington, D.C.: World Bank, 1996.

Collste, Göran. *Makten, Moralen och Människa: En analys av värdekonflikter i debatten om medbestämmande och löntagarstyre.* Uppsala: Acta Universitatis Upsaliensis, 1984.

Dagens Nyheter, 24 August 1996, Stockholm, A21.

Daly, Herman E. *Beyond Growth.* Boston: Beacon Press, 1996.

Daly, Herman E., and John Cobb Jr. *For the Common Good: Redirecting the Economy toward Community, the Environment, and a Sustainable Future.* Boston: Beacon Press, 1989.

Daly, Herman E., and Kenneth N. Townsend, eds. *Valuing the Earth: Economics, Ecology, Ethics.* Cambridge: MIT Press, 1993.

Daly, Lois K., ed. *Feminist Theological Ethics.* Louisville: Westminster John Knox Press, 1994.

Daly, Mary. *Beyond God the Father: Towards a Philosophy of Women's Liberation.* Boston: Beacon Press, 1973.

———. *Gyn/ecology: The Metaethics of Radical Feminism.* Boston: Beacon Press, 1978.

Drèze, Jean, and Amartya Sen. *Hunger and Public Action.* WIDER Studies in Development Economics. Oxford: Clarendon Press, 1989.

Drimmelen Rob van. *Faith in a Global Economy: A Primer for Christians.* Geneva: WCC Publications, 1998.

Duchrow, Ulrich. *Europa i Världssystemet 1492–1992.* Lund, Sweden: Institutet för kontextuell teologi, 1992.

———. *Global Economy: A Confession Issue for the Churches?* Geneva: WCC Publications, 1987.

Eck, Diana L., and Devaki Jain, eds. *Speaking of Faith: Cross-cultural Perspectives on Women, Religion, and Social Change.* London: Women's Press, 1986.

Elson, Diane, ed. *Male Bias in the Development Process.* London: MacMillan, 1991.

Emt, Ewa Jeanette and Elisabeth Mansén, eds. *Feministisk filosofi, en antologi.* Nora, Sweden: Nya Doxa, 1994.

England, Paula. "The Separative Self: Androcentric Bias in Neoclassical Assumptions." In *Beyond Economic Man: Feminist Theory and Economics,* edited by Marianne A. Ferber and Julie A. Nelson. Chicago: Univ. of Chicago Press, 1993.

Eriksson, Anne-Louise. *The Meaning of Gender in Theology: Problems and Possibilities.* Uppsala: Teologiska institutionen, 1995.

Etzioni, Amatai. *The Moral Dimension: Towards a New Economics.* New York: Free Press, 1988.

Fabella, Virginia, and Mercy Amba Oduyoyo, eds. *With Passion and Compassion: Third World Women Doing Theology.* Maryknoll, N.Y.: Orbis Books, 1988.

Feinberg, Joel. *Social Philosophy.* Englewood Cliffs, N.J.: Prentice Hall, 1973.

Ferber, Marianne A., and Julie A. Nelson, eds. *Beyond Economic Man: Feminist Theory and Economics.* Chicago: Univ. of Chicago Press, 1993.

Fiorenza, Elizabeth Schüssler. *In Memory of Her: A Feminist Theological Reconstruction of Christian Origins.* New York: Crossroad, 1983.

Firestone, Shulamith. *The Dialectic of Sex: The Case for Feminist Revolution.* New York: Bantam Books, 1970.

Folbre, Nancy. *Who Pays for the Kids: Gender and the Structure of Constraint.* New York: Routledge, 1994.

————, ed. *The Economics of the Family.* The International Library of Critical Writings in Economics 64. Aldershot, England: Edward Elgar Publishing, 1996.

Föllestad, Dagfinn, Lars Walö, and Jon Elster. *Argumentasjonsteroi, språk og vitenskapsfilosofi.* Oslo: Universitetsforlaget, 1990.

Frank, Robert H., Thomas Gilovich, and Denis T. Regan. "Does Studying Economics Inhibit Cooperation?" *Journal of Economic Perspectives* 7, no. 2 (1993): 159–71.

Fraser, Nancy. "False Antitheses." In *Feminist Contentions: A Philosophical Exchange,* edited by Seyla Benhabib, Judith Butler, Drucilla Cornell, and Nancy Fraser. New York: Routledge, 1995.

————. *Justice Interruptus: Critical Reflections on the "Postsocialist" Condition.* New York: Routledge, 1998.

————. *Unruly Practices: Power, Discourse and Gender in Contemporary Social Theory.* Cambridge, England: Polity Press, 1989.

————. "What's Critical about Critical Theory?" In *Feminists Read Habermas: Gendering the Subject of Discourse,* edited by Johanna Meehan. New York: Routledge, 1995.

Freire, Paulo. *Pedagogy of the Oppressed.* 1968. Reprint, New York: Seabury Press, 1974.

Galbraith, John Kenneth. *A Short History of Financial Euphoria.* New York: Viking Penguin, 1993.

Galtung, Johan. *Theory and Method of Social Research.* Oslo: Universitetsforlaget, 1967.

Gebara, Ivone. *Longing for Running Water: Ecofeminism and Liberation.* Minneapolis: Fortress Press, 1999.

Gerle, Elisabeth. *In Search of a Global Ethics: Theological, Political and Feminist Perspectives Based on a Critical Analysis of JPIC and WOMP.* Lund, Sweden: Lund Univ. Press, 1995.

George, Henry. *Progress and Poverty.* New York: Random House, 1879.

George, Susan. *The Debt Boomerang: How Third World Debt Harms Us All.* London: Pluto Press, 1992.

George, Susan, and Fabrizio Sabelli. *Faith and Credit: The World Bank's Secular Empire.* New York: Penguin Books, 1994.

Gesell, Silvio. *Die natürliche Wirtschaftsordnung.* Verlag: Rudolf Zitzmann, 1949. (ET=*The Natural Economic Order.* 2 vols. San Antonio: Free-Economy Publishing, 1934–36.)

Goldberg, Gertrude Schaffner, and Eleanor Kremen, eds. *The Feminization of Poverty: Only in America?* New York: Praeger Publishers, 1990.

Gorringe, Timothy J. *Capital and the Kingdom: Theological Ethics and Economic Order.* Maryknoll, N.Y.: Orbis Books, 1993.

Grenholm, Carl-Henric. *Christian Social Ethics in a Revolutionary Age.* Stockholm: Verbum, 1973.

———. *Protestant Work Ethics: A Study of Work Ethical Theories in Contemporary Protestant Theology.* Uppsala: Acta Universitatis Upsaliensis, 1993.

Gurr, Ted G. *Why Men Rebel.* Princeton, N.J.: Princeton Univ. Press, 1970.

Gutiérrez, Gustavo. *On Job: God-Talk and the Suffering of the Innocent.* 1987. Reprint, Maryknoll, N.Y.: Orbis Books, 1996.

———. *A Theology of Liberation.* Maryknoll, N.Y.: Orbis Books, 1971.

Harding, Sandra. "Can Feminist Thought Make Economics More Objective?" *Feminist Economics* 1, no. 1 (1995): 7–23.

Harrison, Beverly Wildung. "The Dream of a Common Language." *Annual of the Society of Christian Ethics* (1993): 1–25.

———. "A Feminist Perspective on Moral Responsibility." *Conscience* (1984/85).

———. *Making the Connections.* Edited by Carol S. Robb. Boston: Beacon Press, 1985.

———. *Our Right to Choose: Toward a New Ethic of Abortion.* Boston: Beacon Press, 1983.

———. Review of "Feminism and Process Thought" by Sheila Davany. *Signs* 7, no. 3. (spring 1982): 704-10.

Harrison, Beverly Wildung and Carter Heyward. "Backlash." *Journal of Feminist Studies in Religion* 10, no. 1 (1994): 91–95.

Hartmann, Heidi. "The Family as the Locus of Gender, Class, and Political Struggle: The Example of Housework." *Signs* 6, no 3. (1981): 366–94.

Hartsock, Nancy M. *Money, Sex, and Power: Toward a Feminist Historical Materialism.* Northeastern Series in Feminist Theory. Boston: Northeastern Univ. Press, 1985.

Hausman, Daniel M., and Michael S. McPherson. *Economic Analysis and Moral Philosophy.* Cambridge: Cambridge Univ. Press, 1996.

Hazlitt, Henry. *From Bretton Woods to World Inflation: A Study of Causes and Consequences.* Chicago: Regnery Gateway, 1984.

Hedin, Dag, and Viggo Mortensen ed. 1992:7, "A Just Europe: The Churches' Response to the Ethical Implications of the New Europe." In *Tro & Tanke,* Uppsala: Svenska Kyrkans Forskningsråd.

Held, Virginia. "Feminism and Moral Theory." In *Women and Moral Theory*, edited by Eva F. Kittay and Diana T. Meyers. Totowa, N.J.: Rowman & Littlefield, 1987.

―――. *Feminist Morality: Transforming Culture, Society, and Politics.* Chicago: Univ. of Chicago Press, 1993.

―――. "The Meshing of Care and Justice." *Hypatia* 10, no. 2 (1995): 128–32.

Henderson, Hazel. *Building a Win-Win World: Life beyond Global Economic Warfare.* San Francisco: Berett-Koehler Publishers, 1996.

―――. *Creating Alternative Futures: The End of Economics.* New York: Berkeley Windhover Books, 1978.

―――. *Paradigms in Progress, Life Beyond Economics.* Indianapolis: Knowledge Systems, 1991.

Heyward, Carter. *Our Passion for Justice: Images of Power, Sexuality and Liberation.* New York: Pilgrim Press, 1984.

―――. *Saving Jesus from Those Who Are Right: Rethinking What It Means to Be Christian.* Minneapolis: Fortress Press, 1999.

―――. *Touching Our Strength: The Erotic as Power and the Love of God.* San Francisco: Harper & Row, 1989.

Heyzer, Noeleen. "Increasing Women's Access to Credit in Asia: Achievements and Limitations." In *Gender, Economic Growth, and Poverty: Market Growth and State Planning in Asia and the Pacific*, edited by Noeleen Heyzer and Gita Sen. New Delhi: Kali for Women; Utrecht: International Books, 1994.

Heyzer, Noeleen, and Gita Sen, eds. *Gender, Economic Growth, and Poverty: Market Growth and State Planning in Asia and the Pacific.* New Delhi: Kali for Women; Utrecht: International Books, 1994.

Hobgood, Mary E. *Catholic Social Teaching and Economic Theory: Paradigms in Conflict.* Philadelphia: Temple Univ. Press, 1991.

Holland, Nancy J. *Is Women's Philosophy Possible?* Savage, Md.: Rowman & Littlefield, 1990.

Hoogendijk, Willem. *The Economic Revolution: Towards a Sustainable Future by Freeing the Economy from Money-Making.* London: Green Print, 1991.

Human Rights Watch. *Global Report on Women's Human Rights.* New York: Human Rights Watch, 1995.

Humphries, Jane, ed. *Gender and Economics.* The International Library of Critical Writings in Economics 45. Aldershot, England: Edward Elgar Publishing, 1995.

Hunt, Mary E. "Feminist Liberation Theology: The Development of Method in Construction." Unpublished dissertation, Berkeley, Calif.: Graduate Theological Union, 1980.

Hunt, Mary E. *Fierce Tenderness: A Feminist Theology of Friendship*. New York: Crossroad, 1991.

Illich, Ivan. *Gender*. Stockholm: Liber, 1985.

International Labor Organization. *Employment, Growth, and Basic Needs: A One World Problem*. Geneva: ILO, 1976.

Isasi-Díaz, Ada-María. "The Task of Hispanic Women's Liberation Theology—*Mujeristas: Who We Are and What We Are About*." In *Feminist Theology from the Third World*, edited by Ursula King. London: SPCK, 1994.

Jaggar, Alison M. *Feminist Politics and Human Nature*. Lanham, Md.: Rowman & Littlefield, 1983.

Jaggar, Alison M., and Susan R. Bordo, eds. *Gender/Body/Knowledge: Feminist Reconstructions of Being and Knowing*. New Brunswick, N.J.: Rutgers Univ. Press, 1989.

Jarl, Ann-Cathrin. "Women's Human Rights." In *Women's Human Rights*. LWF Studies. Geneva: Lutheran World Federation, 1984.

Johnston, Carol. *The Wealth or Health of Nations: Transforming Capitalism from Within*. Cleveland: Pilgrim Press, 1998.

Jonásdottir, Anna G. *Love, Power and Political Interests: Towards a Theory of Patriarchy in Contemporary Western Societies*. Örebro, Sweden: Örebro Studies, 1991.

Keller, Catherine. *From a Broken Web: Separation, Sexism and Self*. Boston: Beacon Press, 1986.

Keller, Evelyn Fox. *Reflections on Gender and Science*. New Haven: Yale Univ. Press, 1985.

Kennedy, Margrit. *Interest- and Inflation-Free Money: How to Create an Exchange Medium That Works for Everybody*. Steyerberg: Permakultur InstituteV, 1988.

Keynes, John M. *The General Theory of Employment Interest and Money*. London: Macmillan and Co., 1936.

Khandker, Shahidur R., Baqui Khalily, and Zahed Khan. *Grameen Bank Performance and Sustainability*. World Bank Discussion Papers 306, Washington D.C.: IBRD, 1995.

King, Ursula, ed. *Feminist Theology from the Third World*. London: SPCK, 1994.

Kittay, Eva Feder, and Diana T. Meyers, eds. *Woman and Moral Theory*. Totowa, N.J.: Rowman & Littlefield, 1987.

Kuhn, Thomas. *The Structure of Scientific Revolution*. Chicago: Univ. of Chicago Press, 1962.

Kuiper, Edith, and Jolande Sap, eds. *Out of the Margin: Feminist Perspectives on Economics*. London: Routledge, 1993.

Kymlika, Will. *Contemporary Political Philosophy: An Introduction*. Oxford: Oxford Univ. Press, 1992.

Lakoff, Georg, and Mark Johnson. *Metaphors We Live By*. Chicago: Univ. of Chicago Press, 1980.

Lebacqz, Karen. *Justice in an Unjust World: Foundations for a Christian Approach to Justice*. Minneapolis: Augsburg Publishing House, 1987.

———. *Six Theories of Justice: Perspectives from Philosophical and Theological Ethics*. Minneapolis: Augsburg Publishing House, 1986.

Lipsey, Richard G., Paul N. Courant, Douglas D. Purvis, and Peter O. Steiner. *Economics*. 10th ed. New York: HarperCollins College Publishers, 1993.

Liss, Per-Erik. *Health Care Needs: Meaning and Measurement*. Linköping, Sweden: Tema, 1990.

Lutz, Mark A., and Kenneth Lux. *Humanistic Economics: The New Challenge*. New York: Bootstrap Press, 1988.

Manushi. A journal about women and society, 1978, New Delhi, India.

Maslow, Abraham H. *Towards a Psychology of Being*. New York: Van Nostrand Reinhold Company, 1968.

McCloskey, Deirdre. *The Vices of Economists: The Virtue of the Bourgeoisie*. Amsterdam: Amsterdam Univ. Press, 1996.

Meehan, Johanna, ed. *Feminists Read Habermas: Gendering the Subject of Discourse*. New York: Routledge, 1995.

Meeks, Douglas M. *God the Economist: The Doctrine of God and Political Economy*. Minneapolis: Fortress Press, 1989.

Meeks, J., and Gay Tulip, eds. *Thoughtful Economic Man: Essays on Rationality, Moral Rules and Benevolence*. Cambridge: Cambridge Univ. Press, 1991.

Mies, Maria, and Vandana Shiva. *Ecofeminism*. Halifax: Fernwood Publications; London: Zed Books, 1993.

Míguez Bonino, José. *Doing Theology in a Revolutionary Situation*. Philadelphia: Fortress Press, 1975.

———. *Toward a Christian Political Ethics*. Philadelphia: Fortress Press, 1983.

Mill, John Stuart. *The Subjection of Women*. 1869. Reprint, Cambridge: MIT Press, 1971.

Miranda, José P. *Marx and the Bible: A Critique of the Philosophy of Oppression*. Maryknoll, N.Y.: Orbis Books, 1974.

Mitchell, Juliet. *Woman's Estate*. Harmondsworth, England: Penguin Books, 1971.

———. "Women: The Longest Revolution." *New Left Review* (November/December 1966).

Moon, Bruce E. *The Political Economy of Basic Human Needs.* Ithaca, N.Y.: Cornell Univ. Press, 1991.

Moraga, Cherríe, and Gloria Anzaldúa, eds. *This Bridge Called My Back: Writings by Radical Women of Color.* Watertown, Mass.: Persephone Press, 1981.

Morris, David M. *Measuring the Conditions of the World's Poor: The Physical Quality of Life Index.* New York: Pergamon, 1979.

Morton, Nelle. *The Journey Is Home.* Boston: Beacon Press, 1985.

Mueller-Vollmer, Kurt, ed. *The Hermeneutics Reader.* New York: Continuum, 1997.

Mulholland, Catherine, comp. *Ecumenical Reflections on Political Economy.* Geneva: WCC Publications, 1988.

Murphy, Craig N., and Roger Tooze, eds. *The New International Political Economy.* Boulder, Colo.: Lynne Rienner Publishers, 1991.

Nationalencyklopedin. Vol. 13. Höganäs: Bra Böcker, 1994.

———. Vol. 19. Höganäs: Bra Böcker, 1995.

Neal, Marie Augusta. *A Socio-Theology of Letting Go: The Role of First World Churches Facing Third World Peoples.* New York: Paulist Press, 1977.

Nelson, Julie A. "Economic Theory and Feminist Theory." In *Out of the Margin: Feminist Perspectives on Economics,* edited by Edith Kuiper and Jolande Sap. London: Routledge, 1995.

———. *Feminism, Objectivity, and Economics.* London: Routledge, 1996.

———. "The Study of Choice or the Study of Provisioning? Gender and the Definition of Economics." In *Beyond Economic Man,* edited by Marianne A. Ferber and Julie A. Nelson. Chicago: Univ. of Chicago Press, 1993.

Niebuhr, Reinhold. *Christian Realism and Political Problems.* New York: Scribner, 1953.

———. *Moral Man and Immoral Society.* 1932. Reprint, New York: Scribner, 1960.

Noddings, Nell. *Women and Evil.* Berkeley: Univ. of California Press, 1989.

Nürnberger, Klaus. *Prosperity, Poverty and Pollution: Managing the Approaching Crisis.* Pietermaritzburg, South Africa: Cluster Publications, 1999.

Nussbaum, Martha C., and Amartya Sen, eds. *The Quality of Life.* New York and London: Oxford Univ. Press, 1993.

Oduyoye, Mercy Amba. "Reflections from a Third World Women's Perspective: Women's Experience and Liberation Theologies." In *Feminist Theology from the Third World,* edited by Ursula King. London: SPCK; Maryknoll, N.Y.: Orbis Books, 1994.

Okin, Susan Moller. *Women in Western Political Thought.* Princeton, N.J.: Princeton Univ. Press, 1979.

O'Neill, Onora. "Justice, Gender, and International Boundaries." In *The Quality of Life*, edited by Martha C. Nussbaum and Amartya Sen. Oxford: Oxford Univ. Press, 1993.

Parsons, Susan Frank. *Feminism and Christian Ethics.* New York: Cambridge Univ. Press, 1996.

Pujol, Michèle A. *Feminism and Anti-Feminism in Early Economic Thought.* 1992. Reprint, Cheltenham, England: Edward Elgar Publishing, 1998.

————. "Into the Margin!" In *Out of the Margin*, edited by Edith Kuiper and Jolande Sap. London: Routledge, 1995.

Purvis, Sally B. "Gender Construction." In *Dictionary of Feminist Theologies*, edited by Letty M. Russell and J. Shannon Clarksson. Louisville: Westminster John Knox Press, 1996.

Robb, Carol S. *Equal Value: An Ethical Approach to Economics and Sex.* Boston: Beacon Press, 1995.

————. "Love Your Enemy: Love, Power and Christian Ethics." In *Feminist Theological Ethics*, edited by Lois K. Daly. Louisville: Westminster John Knox Press, 1994.

Robb, Carol S., and Carl J. Casebolt. *Covenant for a New Creation: Ethics, Religion and Public Policy.* Maryknoll, N.Y.: Orbis Books, 1991.

Robertson, James. *Future Wealth: A New Economics for the 21st Century.* New York: Bootstrap Press, 1990.

Rowbotham, Sheila. *Woman's Consciousness, Man's World.* Middlesex, England: Penguin Books, 1973.

Ruether, Rosemary Radford. *Liberation Theology: Human Hope Confronts Christian History and American Power.* New York: Paulist Press, 1972.

————. *New Woman, New Earth: Sexist Ideologies and Human Liberation.* Melbourne: Dove Communications, 1975.

————. *Sexism and God-Talk: Towards a Feminist Theology.* Boston: Beacon Press, 1983.

————. "Women and Culture." *CONSCIENCE* 16, no. 4 (1990).

Russell, Letty M., and J. Shannon Clarksson, eds. *Dictionary of Feminist Theologies.* Louisville: Westminster John Knox Press, 1996.

Ryan, John A. *Economic Justice: Selections from Distributive Justice and a Living Wage*, edited by Harlan R. Beckley. Louisville: Westminster John Knox Press, 1996.

Santa Ana, Julio de. *Good News to the Poor: The Challenge of the Poor in the History of the Church.* Geneva: WCC, 1977.

Schleiermacher, Fredrick D. E. "General Hermeneutics." 1819. Reprinted in *The Hermeneutics Reader*, edited by Kurt Mueller-Vollmer. New York: Continuum, 1997.

Schubeck, Thomas L., S.J. *Liberation Ethics.* Minneapolis: Fortress Press, 1993.

Schumacher, E. F. *A Guide for the Perplexed*. London: Abacus, 1978.

————. *Small Is Beautiful: Economics as if People Mattered*. 1973. Reprint, New York: Harper Perennial, 1989.

Secord, Paul F., and Carl W. Backman. *Social Psychology*. New York: McGraw-Hill Book Company, 1964.

Sedgwick, Peter H. *The Market Economy and Christian Ethics*. Cambridge: Cambridge Univ. Press, 1999.

Sen, Amartya. "Capability and Well-Being." In *The Quality of Life*, edited by Martha C. Nussbaum and Amartya Sen. New York and London: Oxford Univ. Press, 1993.

————. *Inequality Reexamined*. New York: Russell Sage Foundation, 1992.

————. "More Than One Hundred Million Women Are Missing: Women's Survival as a Development Problem." *New York Review of Books* (1990): 61–66.

————. *On Ethics and Economics*. Oxford: Blackwell, 1987.

————. *Poverty and Famine: An Essay on Entitlement and Deprivation*. Oxford: Clarendon Press, 1981.

————. *Resources, Values and Development*. Oxford: Blackwell; Cambridge: Harvard Univ. Press, 1984.

Sen, Gita. "Poverty, Economic Growth, and Gender Equity: The Asian and Pacific Experience." In *Gender, Economic Growth, and Poverty*, edited by Noeleen Heyzer and Gita Sen. New Delhi: Kali for Women; Utrecht: International Books, 1994.

————. "Reproduction: The Feminist Challenge to Social Policy." In *Power and Decision: The Social Control of Reproduction*, edited by Gita Sen and Rachel C. Snow. Harvard Series on Population and International Health. Cambridge: Harvard Univ. Press, 1994.

Sen, Gita, Adrienne Germain, and Lincoln C. Chen, eds. *Population Policies Reconsidered: Health Empowerment and Rights*. Harvard Series on Population and International Health. Cambridge: Harvard Univ. Press, 1994.

Sen, Gita, and Caren Grown, *Development Crises and Alternative Visions: Third World Women's Perspectives*. London: Earthscan Publications, 1987.

Sen, Gita, and Rachel C. Snow, eds. *Power and Decision: The Social Control of Reproduction*. Harvard Series on Population and International Health. Cambridge: Harvard Univ. Press, 1995.

Sivard, Ruth Leger. *World Military and Social Expenditures*. Washington D.C.: World Priorities Inc., 1985.

————. *World Military and Social Expenditures*. Washington D.C.: World Priorities Inc., 1996.

Smith, Adam. *An Inquiry into the Nature and Causes of the Wealth of Nations.* 1776. Reprint, edited by Kathryn Sutherland, Oxford: Oxford Univ. Press, 1993.

———. *The Theory of Moral Sentiments.* 1759. Reprint, edited by D. D. Raphael and A. L. Macfie, Indianapolis: Liberty Fund, 1984.

Solow, Robert M. "Feminist Theory, Women's Experience and Economics." In *Beyond Economic Man,* edited by Marianne A. Ferber and Julie A. Nelson. Chicago: Chicago Univ. Press, 1993.

Soros, George. "Can There Be a Global Economy without a Global Society?" Stockholm: SIPRI, 1998. Mimeograph.

Spero, Joan Edelman. *The Politics of International Economic Relations.* 4th ed. New York: St. Martin's Press, 1990.

Sporre, Karin. *Först när vi får ansikten–ett flerkulturellt samtal om feminism, etik och teologi.* Stockholm: Atlas Akademi, 1999.

Stackhouse, Max L., Peter L. Berger, Dennis P. McCann, and M. Douglas Meeks. *Christian Social Ethics in a Global Era.* Abingdon Press Studies in Christian Ethics and Economic Life 1. Nashville: Abingdon Press, 1995.

Stanton, Elizabeth Cady. *Eighty Years and More, Reminiscences 1815–1897.* 1898. Reprint, New York: Schocken Books, 1971.

Sterba, James P. *Justice for Here and Now.* Cambridge: Cambridge Univ. Press, 1998.

Stewart, Frances. "War and Underdevelopment: Can Economic Analysis Help Reduce the Cost?" *Journal of International Development* 5, no.4 (1993): 357–80.

Streeten, Paul, Shahid Javed Burki, Mahub Ul Haq, Norman Hicks, and Frances Stewart. *First Things First: Meeting Basic Human Needs in the Developing Countries.* Published for the World Bank. New York and Oxford: Oxford Univ. Press, 1981.

Sundman, Per. *Human Rights, Justification, and Christian Ethics.* Uppsala: Acta Universitatis Upsaliensis, 1996.

Tamez, Elsa. *The Amnesty of Grace: Justification by Faith from a Latin American Perspective.* Nashville: Abingdon Press, 1993.

Tickner, Ann J. "On the Fringes of the World Economy: A Feminist Perspective." In *The New International Political Economy,* edited by Craig N. Murphy and Roger Tooze. Boulder, Colo.: Lynne Rienner, Publishers, 1991.

Trible, Phyllis. *Texts of Terror: Literary-Feminist Readings of Biblical Narratives.* Philadelphia: Fortress Press, 1984.

Troeltsch, Ernst. *The Social Teaching of the Christian Churches.* 2 vols. 1923. Reprint, Chicago: Univ. of Chicago Press, 1981.

UNDP. *Human Development Report.* New York: Oxford Univ. Press, 1995.

————. *Human Development Report.* New York: Oxford Univ. Press, 1996.

————. *Human Development Report.* New York: Oxford Univ. Press, 1997.

————. *Human Development Report.* New York: Oxford Univ. Press, 1998.

United Nations. *The Nairobi Forward-Looking Strategies for the Advancement of Women.* New York: United Nations Department of Public Information, 1985.

————. *The World's Women 1995: Trends and Statistics.* New York: United Nations, 1995.

Waltzer, Michael. *Spheres of Justice.* New York: Basic Books, 1983.

Ward, Barbara. *Spaceship Earth.* New York: Columbia Univ. Press, 1966.

Ward, Kathryn. *Women, Workers, and Global Restructuring.* Ithaca, N.Y.: PILR Press, 1990.

Waring, Marilyn. *If Women Counted: A New Feminist Economics.* San Francisco: Harper & Row, 1988.

Welch, Sharon D. *Communities of Resistance and Solidarity: A Feminist Theology of Liberation.* Maryknoll, N.Y.: Orbis Books, 1985.

————. *A Feminist Ethic of Risk.* Minneapolis: Fortress Press, 1990.

————. *Sweet Dreams in America: Making Ethics and Spirituality Work.* New York: Routledge, 1999.

Weston, Burns H., Richard A. Falk, and Anthony D'Amato. *Basic Documents in International Law and World Order.* St. Paul, Minn.: West Publishing Co., 1990.

Wolfensohn, James D. Foreword to *Post-Conflict Reconstruction, the Role of the World Bank.* Washington D.C.: IBRD, 1998.

Wollstonecraft, Mary. *Vindication of the Rights of Woman,* 1772. Reprint, edited by Miriam Kramnick, Miriam, Hamondsworth, England: Penguin Books, 1978.

Woolley, Frances R. "The Feminist Challenge to Neoclassical Economics." In *Gender and Economics,* edited by Jane Humphries. The International Library of Critical Writings in Economics 45. Aldershot, England: Edward Elgar Publishing, 1995.

World Bank. *Advancing Gender Equality: From Concept to Action.* Washington, D.C.: IBRD, 1995.

————. *Gender Issues in World Bank Lending.* Washington, D.C.: IBRD, 1995.

————. *Post-Conflict Reconstruction: The Role of the World Bank.* Washington, D.C.: IBRD, 1998.

————. *Toward Gender Equality: The Role of Public Policy.* Washington, D.C.: IBRD, 1995.

————. *Violence against Women: The Hidden Health Burden.* Washington, D.C.: IBRD, 1994.

————. *Women, Poverty, and Productivity in India.* Washington, D.C.: IBRD, 1992.

————. *The World Bank and the Poorest Countries: Support for Development in the 1990s.* Washington, D.C.: IBRD, 1994.

————. *The World Bank Research Program.* Washington, D.C.: IBRD, 1995.

————. *World Development Indicators.* Washington, D.C.: IBRD, 1998.

Young, Iris Marion. *Justice and the Politics of Difference.* Princeton, N.J.: Princeton Univ. Press, 1990.

Young, Pamela Dickey. *Feminist Theology/Christian Theology: In Search of Method.* Minneapolis: Fortress Press, 1990.

INDEX